BEHAVIORAL THERAPY
FOR
RURAL SUBSTANCE ABUSERS

BEHAVIORAL THERAPY
FOR
RURAL SUBSTANCE ABUSERS

A TREATMENT INTERVENTION
FOR
SUBSTANCE ABUSERS

Carl Leukefeld

Theodore Godlaski

James Clark

Cynthia Brown

Lon Hays

Center on Drug and Alcohol Research
University of Kentucky
Lexington, Kentucky

THE UNIVERSITY PRESS OF KENTUCKY

This manual was developed with funding from the
National Institute on Drug Abuse Grant No. RO 10101

Editorial and Sales Offices: The University Press of Kentucky
663 South Limestone Street, Lexington, Kentucky 40508–4008

04 03 02 01 00   5 4 3 2 1

Library of Congress Cataloging-in-Publication Data

Behavioral therapy for rural substance abusers / Carl Leukefeld . . . [et al.].
    p. cm.
    Includes bibliographical references and index.
    ISBN 0-8131-0984-1 (pbk. : alk. paper)
    1. Substance abuse—Treatment—United States. 2. Rural population—Medical
    care—United States. I. Leukefeld, Carl G.
    RA565.65.B47   2000
    616.86'0651—dc21   99-047768

This book is printed on acid-free recycled paper meeting
the requirements of the American National Standard
for Permanence in Paper for Printed Library Materials.

Manufactured in the United States of America.

CONTENTS

Acknowledgments

The authors wish to thank the participating treatment sites: Adanta Behavioral Health Services, with directors Cathy Epperson and Sherry DeBord, and Kentucky River Community Care, with directors Dr. Louise Howell and Wilma Terry. We are grateful to the therapists who were part of the journey and provided valuable feedback along the way: Mike Dow, Jim Gibson, Missy Herron, Susan Miller, LeAnn Pickett, Terry Stephens, Gary Wallace, and William Wethington.

We would also like to thank Dr. Peter Monti for his insightful consultation and Michele Staton and Lucy Letton who contributed.

Introduction

Rural communities, like urban communities, have drug- and alcohol-related problems (Edward, 1992). Based on information from urban centers, it is evident that therapies cannot be used in rural areas without modification. The characteristics of the substance abuser, drug(s) of choice, and the community where the client lives are important issues to be considered when selecting a therapy. However, there is little information about the changes required for therapies designed for urban populations to make them useful for rural residents (Leukefeld et al., 1992), and only a few studies focus specifically on rural drug treatment (Government Accounting Office, 1990). This manual-driven therapy, called Structured Behavioral Outpatient Rural Therapy (SBORT), builds on what has been learned in rural areas about individual and community characteristics and substance abuse treatment for substance abusers in a rural setting.

This manual has been developed for clinicians who work with drug- and alcohol-abusing clients in rural areas. It is grounded in clinical approaches that have been successful with substance abusers: motivational interviewing, case management, thought mapping, structured storytelling, and social skills training. Motivational interviewing and case management are individual approaches, while social skills training is a group approach. Combining these approaches provides a method for engaging clients in a process of change and growth regarding their relationship with drugs and living.

Structured Behavioral Rural Therapy (SBORT) was developed and piloted over three years by University of Kentucky faculty, staff, and substance abuse counselors in rural Eastern Kentucky, with a grant from the National Institute on Drug Abuse. Focus groups were used initially during a process to select social skills and to modify therapeutic methods and approaches for rural substance abusers. The manual was first piloted in a rural treatment program, and after refinements and input from focus groups, it was piloted at three rural outpatient treatment settings. The manual is grounded in therapeutic approaches that have been successfully used in big cities with substance users but that have not been systematically applied in rural areas. In fact, before SBORT was developed, there was no theoretically grounded therapy we were able to identify that specifically focused on rural substance abusers. SBORT combines individual and group methods, using structured storytelling rather than traditional role-playing.

Motivational interviewing is an individual treatment approach that is designed to help clinicians engage substance abusers in a process of change (Miller and Rollnick, 1991). The underlying assumption is that addicted individuals are ambivalent about changing their drug-using behaviors. The therapist's role is to help the individual resolve his or her ambivalence to determine the best way of changing. Case management is incorporated into the approach and is defined as maintaining contact with the "other parts" of the client's life during treatment in order to help each client access needed services while simultaneously teaching the skills to do so (Siegal et al., 1995).

Social skills training is a treatment approach that targets skill deficits in addicted individuals. The assumption is that drug use and drinking are learned behaviors. The lack of basic social skills creates situations in which individuals are more likely to use substances to relieve discomfort. Social skills training focuses on enhancing skills among addicted individuals (Monti et al., 1989). It is a group approach that uses the group setting to teach and practice new skills.

Structured Behavioral Outpatient Rural Therapy is presented in this manual as an intense two-phase outpatient treatment approach that includes pretreatment and treatment. Individual pretreatment sessions incorporate three individual sessions using motivational interviewing as part of the assessment process to develop an individual behavioral change contract and to begin case management. The social skills treatment phase lasts six weeks with two group sessions scheduled each week. Treatment begins with social skills training sessions that were selected by rural therapists and persons in recovery to be most useful in maintaining recovery. Structured storytelling and thought mapping are used to help rural clients develop and practice skills by targeting their problem behaviors—what came before that behavior and the consequences of the behavior.

Developing the Therapy

This manual was developed and modified using focus groups and individual interviews. Focus group members supported the treatment phases, which include individual sessions and group sessions. Focus groups including rural therapists, agency supervisors, recovering clients, and University clinical faculty were asked to prioritize social skills and to add sessions that could be relevant for rural substance abusers. Using a modified Delphi approach, responses clustered into three areas: (1) Most Important—Anger Management, Problem Solving, Close and Intimate Relationships, Managing Thoughts and Fantasies about Drug Use, Relaxing in Stressful Situations, Increasing Pleasant Activities, and Coping with Cravings and Urges; (2) Important—Assertiveness, Receiving Criticisms, Planning for Emergencies, Relaxation, Anger Awareness, and Enhancing Social Support Networks; (3) Less Important—Non-Verbal Communications, Starting Conversations, Giving Criticisms, Relaxation Practice, Listening Skills, Awareness of Negative Thinking, Refusing a Drug, Giving and Receiving Compliments, Refusal Skills, HIV, and Irrelevant Decisions. Self-Acceptance and Building Self-Esteem were suggested for other social skills sessions.

Focus group participants were also asked to review and make recommendations about the therapeutic process in order to tailor the therapy for rural substance abuse clients. Their recommendations are summarized in the following areas:

Engagement—Friendliness, empathy, and respect were stressed as the most important factors to engage clients. This usually involves behaviors such as welcoming the clients in the waiting room, shaking the client's hand, holding the door open, and inviting the client to enter the office first. Finding common personal interests and experiences were critical for initial engagement.

Motivation—Linking a client's drug use with his or her painful life experiences is essential for motivating change. Giving the client autonomy and control in determining the direction and speed of change is most important for rural clients. Therapists indicated that motivation was linked to client questions and desire to change after associating unpleasant events with drug use. These indicators were motivators for therapists to individualize therapy.

Assessment—Enthusiasm was expressed about structured assessments, and an open-ended format was welcomed. Medical and reproductive questions should be asked carefully. Using a medical checklist was preferred. Questions about family of origin, spirituality, and religion are very important.

Case Management—Therapists reported that case management activities should be used to link clients to community services. A major problem facing rural clients is limited money and personal resources, including transportation. Another issue is low-paying jobs and unemployment. Obtaining a job during the day means clients must stop therapy since many agencies do not have evening hours. Childcare is limited or non-existent. Perceptions of social service agencies are negative, even though some clients' families have relied upon government services and money for generations. There is also limited housing and few local self-help groups in rural areas. Accessibility of services was stressed as most important in the initial steps of recovery. Finally, coaching is usually necessary to help clients.

Thought Mapping—There was general agreement that thought mapping would help relate behavioral causes and effects. It would also be useful for clients with cognitive impairments and for those who do not read well. Mapping will help in teaching decision making to link decisions rather than assume they are separate. There was also agreement that maps should be simple.

Social Skills Training—It was suggested that social skills could be most efficiently taught using structural stories and concrete examples. Skills should also be tailored for rural clients. For example, the close and intimate contacts of men and women in rural areas usually do not include physical or direct expressions of love. In addition, rural males tend to express anger as outrage—otherwise it is usually culturally inappropriate to express anger.

General Issues—Family of origin must be considered in therapy. However, no matter how dysfunctional the family of origin, clients are unlikely to be critical. The autonomy, privacy, and dignity of rural clients must be respected. Concrete examples, personal experiences, and stories are important. Spiritual considerations must be taken into account, which differ for younger and older clients. Clients in treatment are most likely to be rural males with criminal justice involvement.

While rural clients will often enter treatment with multiple problems, including dual diagnosis and child abuse, therapists need to focus on treating problems that represent the current problem, target therapy, and limit risk. Clients include those who need habilitation as well as rehabilitation. Those needing rehabilitation will be most successful with social skills training. Therapists should present themselves as counselors rather than as social change agents. However, contact needs to be maintained with probation and parole agencies to clarify the consequences of decisions to engage, sabotage, or leave treatment.

Recovering persons provided additional feedback to develop SBORT and suggested self-help activities. Recovering persons also stressed incorporating spiritual dimensions of recovery as well as including recovering persons as role models. Recovering persons indicated that it is important not to overwhelm rural clients with too many steps. Social skills should parallel recovery. For example, when sequencing skills sessions, "managing urges and cravings" should be reviewed early in recovery. Rural people relate well to storytelling. Stories should focus on other people who have faced similar situations and difficulties, appropriate therapist self-disclosure stories, and popular culture. Recovering persons also indicated that complete abstinence should not be required as a condition for participation in therapy. Thought mapping should be used throughout the entire process. Simple language should always be used.

Content should be reviewed from previous sessions. Rural males will protect rural females in group sessions. Rural kin and friendship networks should be used positively in groups. Clients should be treated like adults. Materials should be sent home to share with family members.

The following therapeutic approaches were suggested: (1) respect clients regardless of their level of formal education; (2) work from a strengths perspective; (3) avoid teacher-student dynamics; (4) be laid-back; (5) understand and appreciate rural humor; (6) avoid ridicule and sarcasm; (7) use stories, examples, and rural metaphors for teaching and counseling; and (8) communicate non-invasive caring, interest, and enthusiasm for clients and your "job." Finally, the following approaches will alienate rural clients: (1) using jargon and "educated words"; (2) overwhelming clients with paperwork early in the engaging process; (3) stereotyping and depersonalizing clients with preconceived communications; (4) trying to control clients with advice and/or threats; and (5) being humorless and refusing to acknowledge the ironies of life.

The Clinical Approach

The overall clinical approach presented in this manual can be used in different settings. For clients who need more support than can be offered twice each week in an outpatient program, a partial hospital program can be developed. This kind of program could offer two social skills groups daily, which are combined with individual motivational interviewing three times per week. For clients requiring less treatment intensity, this approach can be modified to weekly social skills groups and weekly individual motivational counseling sessions. In other words, the frequency of treatment should be determined by client needs.

The clinical intervention is presented in this manual as a two-phase intensive outpatient program.

Phase I: Pretreatment incorporates assessment and evaluation, treatment engagement, motivational interviewing, and case management principles. Clients are seen individually for at least three sessions for 50 minutes each. A therapist works with the client so they both can gain an understanding of the reality that substances play in the client's life and come to a joint commitment for change. During this phase, the therapist adopts the role of facilitator and case manager—a role that will continue throughout treatment.

Phase II: Treatment begins with social skills training, which focuses on those social skills most helpful in establishing and maintaining recovery from chemical dependency. This group approach uses storytelling, thought mapping, and role-playing as methods for assisting clients in developing the skills presented. The entire phase takes about six weeks. A client attends group sessions two times a week and is seen individually for 50 minutes at least three times in six weeks continuing the motivational interviewing approach.

Time Frame

The following time frame presents an overview of the approach highlighting the two phases: pretreatment and treatment. Phase I consists of three individual assessment sessions in a two-week period. Phase II consists of twelve social skills sessions and at least three individual sessions during the six-week period. It is recommended that drug testing be used throughout the time period.

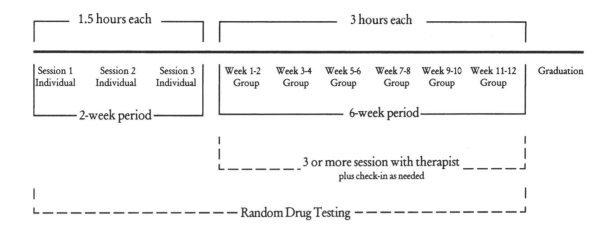

Figure 1.1 *Time frame for Structured Behavioral Outpatient Rural Therapy (SBORT)*

Overview of SBORT

After this introduction to SBORT, which has briefly described the approach used to develop this therapy, the rest of the manual describes the specific methods used in the manual as well as related issues. The manual follows with a description of motivational interviewing, developed by Miller and Rollnick (1991), which is based on the stages of change outlined by Prochaska and DiClemente (1982). For SBORT, motivational interviewing focuses on the therapist's summarizing client statements and asking open-ended questions to help clients make their own decisions. The three pretreatment and assessment sessions focus on obtaining individual client information with a structured series of open-ended questions to assure that a comprehensive assessment is completed, using motivational interviewing to "motivate" clients to remain in treatment. Three therapist issues are introduced that are important for pretreatment sessions as well as the group social skills sessions: (1) Risk Management, (2) Dual Relationships, and (3) Supervision. The strengths-based case management approach (Rapp, 1992) is also presented, which, as implied, focuses on clients' strengths rather than their problems. Long-term behavioral change contracts are also incorporated. Thought mapping is presented as an approach used in social skills sessions to help clients "look at" the consequences of their behavior, particularly problem behavior, as well as what came before their problem behavior—antecedents—and what came after their behavior—consequences. Thought mapping is a visual way of looking at behavior, using what can be called a "road map."

Structured storytelling is also included as part of the group social skills sessions. Structured storytelling or "Priming the Pump" is used in SBORT to reinforce specific social skills being taught by the therapist rather than role-playing. After group participants are asked to present their own stories relevant to the specific social skill, "Prime the Pump" stories are used to stimulate related individual participant stories. Finally, twelve group social skills sessions are outlined (Monti et al., 1989) which incorporate thought mapping and structured storytelling. These sessions are presented as didactic interactive sessions. This is the Structured Behavioral Outpatient Rural Therapy in a nutshell. It has been piloted in three rural Kentucky sites with many revisions and a lot of discussion. Most of the rural therapists involved were comfortable with SBORT. We hope other rural therapists also find it useful.

Motivational Interviewing

Motivational interviewing is the approach used throughout SBORT to engage clients. It is based on the logic that any change in human behavior, including the changes that lead from substance abuse and dependency to recovery, is based on a process of change described by Prochaska and DiClemente (1982). The process involves distinct stages that therapists can use as a framework to assess clients' status and to help clients move forward in the change process. This theory of change was modified by Miller and Rollnick (1991) to include relapse as part of the change process and is represented by the figure below (Figure 1.2).

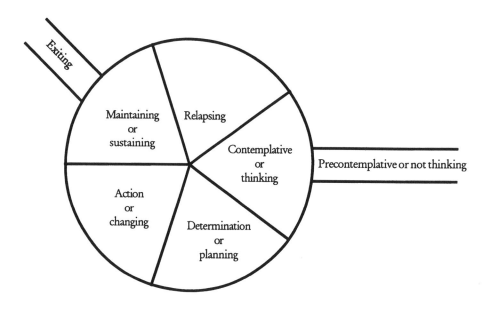

Figure 1.2 *Transtheoretical model of change (Adapted from Prochaska & DiClemente, 1982)*

[The section that follows is adapted from Miller, W., Zweben, A., DiClemente, C., Rychtarik, R. (1994). *Motivational Enhancement Therapy Manual: A Clinical Research Guide for Therapists Treating Individuals with Alcohol Abuse and Dependence.* NIH Publication No. 94--723; U.S. Department of Health and Human Services; Rockville, Md. It is suggested that therapists also read Miller, W. & Rollnick, S. (1991). *Motivational Interviewing: Preparing People to Change Addictive Behavior.* The Guilford Press: New York (3--157).]

Figure 1.2 illustrates the transtheoretical model of change developed by Prochaska and DiClemente (1982), which was modified by Miller and Rollnick (1991). According to this approach, a person begins outside the change cycle in a "precontemplative" or "not thinking about changing" state. At this point in the change process, an individual has a problem with alcohol or drugs but does not know it. She may be aware of various problems in her life but does not associate these problems with the use of substances. As the individual begins to recognize that the use of substances is associated with various problems, she enters the "contemplative," or "thinking about changing," stage of the change cycle. During this stage, ambivalence about change is normal. The desire for positive change and the desire to maintain the status quo alternate in the substance abuser's mind, sometimes moment by moment. As the balance shifts toward positive change, the substance abuser "moves" toward the stage of "determination" or "planning for change." In the determination stage, a substance abuser must formulate a plan of change that is acceptable, workable, appropriate, and effective (Miller & Rollnick, 1991). The determination stage may be a window of opportunity for moving from thinking about a problem to doing something about it.

This window of opportunity for change appears to be time limited. However, it is important that individuals have sufficient time and encouragement to plan positive change. The more thoughtful, concrete, and specific the plan, the more likely successful change will occur. If a workable plan is not formulated, the individual moves back to a contemplative stage. When a substance abuser puts her plan into effect, she enters the "action" or "changing" stage. This stage involves specific changes in a variety of behaviors that move the substance abuser away from using alcohol and/or drugs toward abstinence and positive coping patterns. Once change is initiated regarding a number of behaviors, it usually continues over time. When this stage is reached, a substance abuser enters the "maintenance" or "sustaining change" stage. During this stage of change, the new behavior, together with all the behaviors that support it, are more "normal" and more comfortable.

Initial behavioral change generally involves a different set of skills than those necessary for maintaining that change over time (Marlatt and Gordon, 1985). If a sufficiently comprehensive change can be maintained, a substance abuser can exit the change cycle for a specific problem behavior. Frequently this does not occur and a substance abuser enters a "relapse" stage in which the change plan collapses and the problematic behavior—substance abuse/dependency—returns. When this happens, a substance abuser must continue through the cycle, examining why the initial plan did not succeed or was not maintained. This leads to new determination, action, and maintenance.

Motivational interviewing does not focus on the origin or cause of abuse or dependency. Substance abuse behaviors are approached in the same way that any harmful or unproductive behavior might be viewed. This conceptualization implies that the client is primarily working against her own resistance. The process is natural and understandable rather than pathological. A client is not obliged to adopt one specific way of seeing or defining her experience or problem. The way of understanding that leads to change is the one that is encouraged. The therapist's role is first to do nothing that will increase resistance and then do what will increase a client's sense of self-efficacy. Thus, it is the client rather than the therapist who holds the keys to her own freedom from substance abuse and dependency. This requires therapeutic strategies that are different from the confrontational posture that has often been part of substance abuse counseling. A therapist's tasks are also different. These tasks, developed by Miller and Rollnick (1991), are summarized for each stage of change in Figure 1.3.

Although there are a number of skills that can be used as part of motivational interviewing, to successfully implement the treatment approach presented in this manual, there are two which we believe are essential: open-ended questioning and summarizing feedback. These two skills are described in this section of the manual along with a variety of other therapeutic skills that are consistent with motivational interviewing. Other motivational interviewing skills are helpful and should be used if

CHANGE STAGE	THERAPIST TASKS	POSSIBLE METHODS
Precontemplation	Raise doubt, increase the client's perception of the risks and problems associated with current behaviors	Open-ended assessment questions, summarizing feedback, which links problematic behavior with substance use
Contemplation	Move the balance in favor of change: raise reasons for change, emphasize the risks of not changing, reinforce the client's sense of self-efficacy	Decisional Balance Worksheet, focused open-ended questions, asking what is needed to bring about incremental change, storytelling
Determination	Assist the client in developing a plan for bringing about desired change; focus the client on concrete, specific, and effective strategies	Storytelling, giving advice and making suggestions using a menu of options, using thought mapping to clarify the links between substance use and other behaviors
Action	Assist the client in taking specific behavioral steps toward the desired change; reinforce positive movement	Case management, recognizing incremental change, focused open-ended questions about the benefits of positive change
Maintenance	Assist the client in developing strategies to prevent relapse	Recognition of the benefits of positive change, identification of other problems which could subvert positive change
Relapse	Assist the client in reviewing the stages of contemplation, determination, and action in order to develop new plans without becoming demoralized or discouraged	Focused open-ended questions about the relapse process, use of thought mapping to explore relapse and set the stage for deliberation

Figure 1.3 *Based on Miller and Rollnick (1991)*

counselors feel comfortable with them. Open-ended questioning and summarizing feedback are essential for the assessment approach presented in Phase I of SBORT treatment. These same skills are important in negotiating behavioral contracts, completing strengths-based case management, and directing discussion in social skills training groups.

Motivational interviewing is an approach that recognizes that individuals do not change as the result of a therapeutic intervention but as a result of assessing their own experience and making appropriate decisions (Miller & Rollnick, 1991). Among common elements with other therapies are the value of assessment and feedback (Kristenson et al., 1983; Miller & Sovereign, 1989; Orford & Edwards, 1977); emphasis on the client's responsibility for change (Edwards & Orford, 1977; Heather, Whitton, & Robertson, 1986; Miller, Gribskov, & Mortell, 1981); the value of clear advice (Edwards et al., 1977;

Kristenson et al., 1983; Chafetz, 1961; Elvy et al., 1988); offering a variety of possible approaches to a problem rather than insisting on one approach (Deci, 1980; Kopel & Arkowitz, 1975; Miller, 1985); the use of therapist empathy (Miller et al., 1980; Valle, 1981); and reinforcement of the client's self-efficacy (Frank, 1973; Miller, 1985; Leake & King, 1977). Motivational interviewing is used to assist an individual to come to terms with his or her own experience.

Because of the assumptions incorporated into motivational interviewing, some therapists will find it easier to use this approach (Miller & Rollnick, 1991: 159). The therapist qualities for motivational interviewing are:

- A respect for individual differences

  Therapists who feel comfortable with the fact that other people may have attitudes, beliefs, and values different from their own and who are comfortable discussing those attitudes, beliefs, and values with others without the need to argue or persuade will be more comfortable using motivational interviewing techniques. Therapists who have a strong investment in a specific set of attitudes, beliefs, or values to the point that they find it uncomfortable relating to those who have different or even opposite views of life are likely to have difficulty with the nonjudgmental approach of motivational interviewing.

- Tolerance for disagreement and ambivalence

  Therapists who are not taken aback when clients disagree with them and who recognize that client ambivalence about change is normal and acceptable will feel more comfortable with motivational interviewing. Conversely, therapists who react negatively when clients disagree with them or who insist that clients maintain a consistent commitment to positive change may have difficulty with a motivational interviewing approach.

- Patience with gradual progress

  Therapists who are comfortable with gradual client progress toward a desired goal and with incremental change will feel more at ease with a motivational interviewing approach. Therapists who have an "all-or-nothing" approach to client change may not feel that a motivational interviewing tactic is effective.

- A genuine interest in and care for clients as individuals

  Therapists who find their clients interesting as people and who have a desire to know about their experiences in other areas are more likely to find motivational interviewing useful. On the other hand, therapists who tend to see their role as one of treating a disease and who see clients as problems may have problems with motivational interviewing.

Recovering rural therapists can face a special challenge, particularly if the therapist actively participates in AA or other self-help groups. Therapists may be under pressure (from themselves and others) to provide only one treatment approach—the modality that worked in their own recovery. This can prevent the clinician from acquiring new treatment skills in order to develop interventions that can be flexibly delivered. This "one size fits all" belief usually results in significant treatment dropout, since no one treatment approach can meet everyone's recovery needs. This problem increases for those rural therapists who do not have access to clinical supervision, continuing education, or training. These therapists may see how they practice therapy as the ultimate statement of who they are as persons. These therapists also may see change as disloyal to the recovering community. This attitude increases when the therapist is geographically and psychologically isolated from other points of view.

Motivational interviewing begins with the assumption that the responsibility and the capacity for change lie with the client. The task of the therapist is to create an environment that will enhance the client's own motivation for and commitment to change. Rather than relying on the therapeutic environment, the therapist seeks to mobilize the client's inner resources as well as encouraging her to use those supportive relationships. The therapist's actions are always directed at increasing the probability that the client will undertake, sustain, and successfully complete a plan of positive change.

Miller and Rollnick have identified *five basic principles* to guide this approach.

1. Express Empathy

    In motivational interviewing the therapist seeks to communicate respect for the client. All communications that imply a superior/inferior relationship are avoided. The therapist's role is supportive and one of consultant. The client's freedom of choice and self-direction are respected to the point that it is clear that only the client can make a decision to change drug-using behavior and carry out that change. The therapist seeks ways to compliment and build up rather than to criticize and tear down. Much of motivational interviewing is listening rather than telling. Any persuasion used is gentle, subtle, and always done with the clear understanding that the client is in charge of his/her own process of change. Reflective listening (accurate empathy) is a key to motivational interviewing. It communicates an acceptance of clients as they are while supporting them in a process of change.

2. Develop Discrepancy

    Motivation for change occurs when people perceive a discrepancy between where they are and where they want to be. Motivational interviewing focuses the client's attention on such discrepancies that arise as a result of drug-using behavior. Early in the change process it may be necessary for the therapist to raise the client's awareness of the negative consequences of drug use in order to assist the client in perceiving the discrepancies that exist. Awareness of such discrepancies allows the client to move toward a frank discussion of the changes required to lessen these discrepancies and allows the client to feel more comfortable.

3. Avoid Argumentation

    Handled poorly, ambivalence and discrepancies can resolve into defensive coping strategies that lessen the client's discomfort but do nothing to change the drug-using behavior. An attack on the drug-using behavior tends to provoke a defensive response from the client and communicates to that the therapist does not really understand. Motivational interviewing specifically avoids all argumentation that increases defensiveness. No attempt is made to have the client accept or admit to any specific diagnostic label. The therapist does not seek to convince or prove by force of argument. Instead, the therapist employs other strategies to assist the client in seeing the consequences of the drug-using behavior and to devalue the perceived importance of the drug-induced experience. Properly conducted, motivational interviewing has the client—not the therapist—state the arguments in favor of change.

4. Roll with Resistance

How the therapist understands and deals with resistance is a defining characteristic of motivational interviewing. In motivational interviewing, therapists do not meet resistance head-on but rather roll with its force, attempting to shift the client's perspective in the process. Ambivalence is seen as a normal part of the change process, and new ways of thinking about problems are invited, not imposed. Ambivalence is openly discussed. Solutions are most often evoked from the client and not imposed by the therapist. A variety of forms of reflective listening are employed for this purpose and will be discussed later in the section on Strategies.

5. Support Self-Efficacy

People who have come to see that they have a serious problem will still not move toward change if they do not believe that specific change is possible for them. Self-efficacy is a critical determinant in behavioral change (Bandura, 1977). In essence, self-efficacy is the belief that one can perform a particular behavior or accomplish a specific task. In this case, it is necessary that clients be persuaded that they can change their drug-using behavior and thus reduce its consequences. Overall optimism is not required; what is necessary is that the client believes that a specific drug-using behavior can be changed. Unless this element is present, the awareness of discrepancy will be resolved into defensive coping, which may lessen the client's discomfort, but which will do nothing to change the drug-using behavior. If one has no hope that things can change, there is little reason to confront a problem.

Strategies for Motivating Change

In early motivational interviewing, strategies focus on developing clients' motivation to change their drug-using behavior. Some clients may enter treatment with significant awareness of the problems caused by their drug use and with determination to change. Other clients enter treatment with little awareness of the problems posed by their drug use and are quite defensive about it. In both cases, opening strategies, which are designed to tip the scales in favor of change, should be used. In the case of an already motivated client, this tests the depth of motivation and strengthens it. In the case of an unaware client, it establishes an awareness of discrepancy on which motivation can build.

SELF-MOTIVATING STATEMENTS

Motivational psychology has demonstrated that when we begin to talk about something in a different way, our beliefs and behaviors begin to change similarly. If a client can hear herself talking about change, and no one has put the word in her mouth, then she can believe that change is the desirable option. If the above is true, then the worst sort of persuasive strategy is one of confrontation.

In motivational interviewing, the therapist focuses on statements that represent movement toward change. Such statements include:

- Being open to input about drug use;

- Acknowledging real or potential problems related to drug use;

- Expressing a need, desire, or willingness to change.

One way to elicit such self-motivating statements is to ask for them, using open-ended statements or questions.

- I assume from the fact that you are here that you have some concerns or difficulties about your drug use. Tell me about these.

- Tell me a little about your drug use. What do you like about using drugs? What's the positive side of drug use for you? What's the other side of the coin? What are some of your worries about drug use?

- Tell me what you've noticed about your drug use over time. How has it changed? What things have you noticed that may concern you or which you think might pose potential problems?

- What have other people told you about your drug use? What are other people worried about?

- What makes you think that you might need to make a change in your drug use?

These questions can be used initially with a client or can be added to the evaluation, which is presented later. Once you get going with the client, simply explore aspects of experience with drugs in various areas of his life. Using open-ended questions and statements best does this. Likewise, when talking about various problem areas in the client's life, ask about the client's perception about a connection between problems with finances, personal relationships, employment, and use of drugs.

Occasionally, therapists may encounter special difficulty in eliciting any self-motivating statements from particular clients. In such cases, another strategy to employ is the use of gentle paradox. In this strategy the therapist voices the client's resistance in an attempt to allow the client to take the other side. This approach should be used with some caution and should be attempted only by therapists who can do it comfortably without sarcasm. Here are some examples.

- You haven't convinced me yet that you are seriously concerned. We have been working through the assessment process now for some time. Is that all you're concerned about?

- I'll tell you one concern that I have. This program is one that requires a fair amount of motivation from people, and frankly, from what you've told me so far, I'm not convinced that you're motivated enough to carry through with it. Are you sure that you want to continue?

- I'm not sure how much you are interested in changing your drug use. It sounds like you might be happier just continuing on as you have before.

Likewise, a client may change an opinion if you state it in an extreme form.

- So using drugs is really important to you. Tell me about that.

- What is it exactly about drug using that you have to hang on to, that you can't seem to let go of?

In general, however, it is always best not to have to use these strategies. Without a doubt, the best way to get a self-motivating statement is to ask for it.

- Tell me what concerns you about your drug use.

- Tell me what it has cost you.

- Tell me why you think it needs to change.

LISTENING WITH EMPATHY

The way a therapist responds to what the client has to say is critical in motivational interviewing. The optimal response is accurate empathy (reflective listening or active listening). In this style of interaction, the therapist listens carefully to the client and then reflects the statement back to the client in a slightly modified or reframed form. This way of responding offers the following advantages:

- It is unlikely to evoke client resistance.

- It encourages the client to keep talking and exploring the topic.

- It communicates respect and caring, building a working therapeutic alliance.

- It clarifies for the therapist exactly what the client means.

- It can be used to reinforce ideas expressed by the client.

This last point is especially important in motivational interviewing. The therapist uses reflective statements selectively to reinforce the client's self-motivating statements. The therapist thus can direct the interaction in a way that reinforces the intent of the client to change and, in doing so, increases the probability that the client will move toward productive change. Further, such selective reflection encourages the client to elaborate on her initial self-motivating statement.

Here is an example of reflection.

> THERAPIST: What else concerns you about your drug use?
> CLIENT: Well, I'm not sure I'm concerned about it, but I do sometimes wonder if I'm using too much.
> THERAPIST: Too much for . . .

CLIENT: For my own good, I guess. It's not like it's really serious, but sometimes I feel really awful, and I can't think straight some of the time.

THERAPIST: It messes up your thinking, your concentration.

CLIENT: Yes, and sometimes I have trouble remembering things.

THERAPIST: And you wonder if that might be because you're using too much.

CLIENT: Well, I know it is sometimes.

THERAPIST: You're pretty sure about that, but maybe there's more.

CLIENT: Yeah, sometimes even when I'm not doing anything I mix things up, and I wonder about that.

THERAPIST: Wonder if . . .

CLIENT: If the drugs aren't frying my brain.

THERAPIST: You think that that can happen to people, maybe to you.

CLIENT: Well, can't it? It's like that old ad with the egg and the frying pan. "Here's your brain on drugs."

THERAPIST: Yes, well I can see how you might be worried.

CLIENT: But I don't think that I'm an addict or anything.

THERAPIST: You don't think that you're an addict, but you do think that you might be overdoing it and damaging yourself in the process.

CLIENT: Yeah.

THERAPIST: Kind of a scary thought. What else worries you?

Reflective listening is not the only strategy used in motivational interviewing, but it is a central one. It is not easy to practice this skill consistently. A therapist must listen closely to the verbal and nonverbal expressions of the client, formulate reflective statements at the appropriate level of complexity, and constantly adjust hypotheses about the client's meaning and state of mind to do it well. Optimal reflective listening suspends advice, agreement, disagreement, suggestions, warnings, teaching, and questions in favor of continued exploration of the client's own process.

In working with clients who are ambivalent, therapists should reflect both sides of the ambivalence. When only one side is reflected ("So you can see that your drug use is causing some problems."), it may cause the client to reinforce the other ("Well, I don't think I have any problem, really."). In such cases, it is always best to use a two-sided reflection:

- You don't think that your drug use is a problem right now, and at the same time, you worry that it could get out of hand and cause some problems in the future.

- You really like using drugs and don't like the idea of giving them up, and you can also see that they are causing some problems with your girlfriend and with your job.

QUESTIONS

In motivational interviewing, opened-ended questions are used to assist the client in exploring various experiences. The evaluation format presented in this manual uses such questions to explore many areas of the client's life experience. Open-ended questions can also be used to invite the client to explore possible solutions to perceived problems. Such questions can be used in the evaluation of Phase I and after giving feedback to the client to get a commitment for continued treatment. They are also helpful in case management to encourage clients to express acceptable solutions to problems that may interfere with treatment or with change.

FEEDBACK

In motivational interviewing, the therapist gives the client summarizing feedback at critical points in the therapeutic interaction. Such summarizing feedback allows the client to see her experiences compressed. When therapists use this technique, they should also attempt to make connections between the client's experience and her drug-using behavior. This allows the client to begin to make connections between experiences, problems, and drug use. The therapist should be careful not to force these connections but to point them out from the information that the client has provided. The assessment format provided in this manual helps therapists to stop at the end of each section to provide summarizing feedback.

These interactions can raise the client's awareness of the role of drug use in life. Positive change and growth is facilitated when we can see that certain activities are consistently associated with desirable outcomes while others are consistently associated with undesirable ones.

Feedback should be offered in the form of a reflective response that seeks to determine the accuracy of the therapist's perception. For example:

- Let me make sure that I have understood what you told me. You started using drugs when you were thirteen. At first you occasionally smoked marijuana with your older brother and some of his friends, but by the time you were fourteen you were using it daily and selling marijuana to supply yourself. At about the same time your grades started to suffer, and you got in trouble for possession at school, so you dropped out by the time you were fifteen. All of this caused a lot of conflict with your parents, so you left home and went to live with your older brother. When you couldn't find a job, one of his friends turned you on to dealing crack. You started using crack as well as dealing it, and when you were sixteen, you got arrested for possession with intent and spent two years in a juvenile lockup. When you got out, you went straight for about six months, but the best job you could find was minimum wage, so you went back to dealing. For the last four years, you've been dealing, using, and working various low-wage jobs. Two weeks ago you were arrested for possession as the result of a traffic stop, and you came to treatment on the advice of your attorney. Does that sound about right to you?

- Let me make sure that I understand what you have told me about your relationship with your wife. You met your wife through a mutual friend. You both liked to drink, smoke marijuana, and party. After a few months of going together, you married and moved into an apartment. Everything seemed to be going fine for the first year of your marriage: you both worked and spent your weekends partying with friends. When your wife became pregnant, she stopped using and didn't want to go out partying with you anymore. This became a source of conflict because you didn't feel that you should stay at home simply because she wanted to. Things got worse after your daughter was born. You felt that so much of your wife's time was taken up with the baby that there was nothing much for you at home. You started going out during the week, drinking and using and would often come home very late. Your wife started to complain about your drinking and drug use, especially after you lost your job because of unexcused absence from work. While you were unemployed for two months, you spent money on drugs that was needed for paying the utility bills. When your wife discovered that the electric company was threatening to shut off service, she left with the baby and moved in with her family. She told you that unless you did something about your drinking and drugging, she would file for divorce. At that point you decided to come here and talk to me about what's going on in your life. Do I have it?

As the therapist offers summarizing feedback, he/she should watch the client's reaction. Clients often may be surprised when they hear a large piece of their life experience condensed into a few sentences. They may find it difficult to accept the clear relationships among various problems in their lives and their use of drugs. Therapists should reflect back the affect that they observed.

- This seems pretty difficult for you to hear.

- You seem surprised by what I just said.

- You're shaking your head. Did I get something wrong or misunderstand something that you've told me?

AFFIRM THE CLIENT

In motivational interviewing, the therapist seeks opportunities to compliment and affirm the client. Recognizing the client's sincerity in seeking answers to the problem of her life, having the courage to confront a difficult situation, or being willing to look at alternate approaches to a problem are all things the therapist should affirm. Such affirmation serves multiple purposes:

- Strengthening the working relationship between therapist and client

- Enhancing the client's sense of empowerment and personal responsibility

- Reinforcing the client's efforts and self-motivating statements

- Supporting the client's self-esteem

DEALING WITH RESISTANCE

In all clinical work, therapists must deal with resistance. In certain clinical approaches resistance is seen as a characteristic of the client or a characteristic of the client's addiction. In motivational interviewing resistance is a reality: it is the client's response to something that the therapist is doing. This view is based on research that shows no significant personality differences between addicted and non-addicted individuals as well as other studies that indicate that different therapeutic styles provoke different degrees of resistance in clients. In motivational interviewing, client resistance is the therapist's problem.

There are certain responses to client resistance that are very likely to evoke even stronger and more rigid resistance. The following types of responses are avoided in motivational interviewing:

- Arguing, disagreeing, challenging

- Judging, criticizing, blaming

- Warning of negative consequences

- Seeking to persuade with logic or evidence

- Interpreting or analyzing the "reasons" for resistance

- Confronting with authority

- Using sarcasm or disbelief

A central goal in motivational interviewing is to assist the client in making self-motivating statements. Such statements include, "I have a problem" and "I need to do something about it." Some responses that can deflect resistance and may lead toward self-motivating statements follow:

- Simple Reflection

  Sometimes simply reflecting back to the client about what he is saying can provoke the client to take the opposite side and balance the picture.

- Reflection with Amplification

  This is a simple modification in which the therapist reflects back what the client is saying but in a slightly amplified or exaggerated way. Therapists must be careful not to overdo the amplification or the client is likely to hear it as sarcasm and respond with hostility.

  CLIENT: But I'm not an addict or anything like that.
  THERAPIST: You don't want to be labeled.
  CLIENT: No, I don't think I have a problem with drugs.
  THERAPIST: So as far as you can see, you really haven't experienced any harm or problems as a result of your drug use.
  CLIENT: Well, I wouldn't say that, exactly.
  THERAPIST: So you think that sometimes your drug use has caused problems but you don't like being called an addict.

- Double-Sided Reflection

  The last statement in the example above is a double-sided reflection. The therapist reflects back both the resistance and the other side of the issue that was discussed earlier in a session.

  CLIENT: But I can't stop using marijuana. I mean all of my friends smoke.
  THERAPIST: You can't imagine how you could not smoke marijuana with your friends, but at the same time you worry about the effect it is having on you.

- Shifting Focus

Another strategy for dealing with resistance is to move the attention away from the area of resistance. This is especially useful if the resistance is the result of the client confronting an issue that he is not yet ready to address.

CLIENT: But I can't stop using marijuana. All of my friends smoke.
THERAPIST: You're getting way ahead of things. I'm not talking about your quitting marijuana here, and I don't think that you should get stuck on that concern right now. Let's just stick with what we're doing here—reviewing your experience—and later on you can decide what, if anything, you want to do about your use of marijuana.

- Rolling with Resistance

Sometimes resistance can be met by moving with it. There is a paradoxical element to this that can often bring a client back to a more balanced view. This can be especially effective with clients who present in a highly oppositional manner and who reject every idea or suggestion.

CLIENT: But I can't stop using marijuana. I mean all of my friends' smoke.
THERAPIST: And it may very well be that when we're through, you'll decide that it's worth it to keep on using marijuana as you have been. It may be just too difficult to make a change. That will be up to you.

REFRAMING

Reframing is a strategy in which the therapist invites the client to examine experiences in a new or reorganized way. When done well, new meaning is given to what has been said. Tolerance is a good example. Many addicts are proud of the fact that they can use large amounts of a drug and still function or that they can use doses of a drug that would be fatal to a normal person. However, this can also be seen as a vulnerability, since the normal defenses of the body that signal when enough of an intoxicant has been taken have been disabled or may have never functioned properly. This leaves the individual more vulnerable to dependence and to the damaging effects of various drugs on the tissues of the body.

Reframing can move clients toward taking action to resolve problems. By placing the problems in a more positive or optimistic light, the therapist also communicates that the problem is solvable and that the client has adequate internal resources. Therapists use reframing to examine the client's own words, views, and perceptions. Here are some examples.

- Drug use as a reward: "You may have a need to reward yourself on the weekend for successfully handling a stressful and difficult job during the week." The implication here is that there may be other ways the client can reward himself.

- Drug use as a protective function: "You don't want to impose additional stress on your family by openly sharing difficulties or concerns in your life like the pain your arthritis gives you or your feelings of depression at being dependent on others. As a result, you carry all of this yourself and try to relieve the tension by using painkillers as a way of trying not to burden your family." The implication here is that the opiate addict has inner strength or reserve, is concerned about family, and could discover other ways to deal with these issues besides using drugs.

- Drug use as an adaptive function: "Your use of drugs can be a way of avoiding conflict or tension in your marriage. Your use of sedatives tends to keep the status quo to keep things as they are. It seems you have been taking drugs to keep your marriage intact. Yet both you and your husband seem uncomfortable with this arrangement." The implication is that the client cares about her marriage and has been trying to keep it together but needs to find a more effective method to accomplish this.

Reframing often has the paradoxical effect of moving the client toward change even though it places the problem behavior in a positive light.

Strategies for Strengthening Commitment

Once the decisional balance has tipped in favor of change, and the client has developed sufficient motivational impetus, therapists need a different set of strategies to consolidate the movement toward change. These strategies are geared toward moving the client into a planning and action change stage. Timing is important to shift from one set of strategies to another. Although there may not be a clear and specific point at which clients move from one stage of change to another, there are indications that a change in therapist strategy is needed.

- The client stops resisting and raising objections.

- The client asks fewer questions about problems and more questions about possible solutions.

- The client appears to be more settled, resolved, unburdened, or peaceful.

- The client makes self-motivating statements about the need to make changes.

- The client begins to imagine how life might be different if change occurred.

The following questions can help determine a client's readiness to accept, continue in, and benefit from further counseling. Conversely, these issues can also be used to recognize individuals who may be at risk of prematurely withdrawing from treatment (Zweben et al., 1988).

- Has the client missed previous appointments without notice or rescheduling?

- If the client was coerced into treatment, has he discussed feelings and reactions to this involuntariness: anger, relief, confusion, resentment, etc.?

- Does the client display hesitancy or indecisiveness about participating in future sessions?

- Is the current treatment quite different from what the client expected? If so, have the client's reactions to the current treatment been discussed?

- Does the client seem to be guarded during sessions or otherwise hesitant or resistant when any suggestion is offered?

- Does the client perceive participation in treatment as a degrading experience rather than an opportunity for an improved life?

If the answers to these questions suggest that the client is not motivated for change, then strategies for strengthening commitment are premature. In such cases, continued use of the strategies, described earlier in this manual, is appropriate.

It is important to note that even when a client is motivated to change, ambivalence will still be present. In the change process, ambivalence is a factor until the change occurs and the benefits of change are clear. Therapists need to recognize this and not press for too much change too soon. It is necessary for the therapist to take the lead from the client and create an atmosphere in which the client feels comfortable talking openly. Sooner or later, however, the therapist will have to move to the strategies discussed in this section of the manual.

DISCUSSING A PLAN
The shift at this time is from a focus on the reasons for change to negotiating a change plan. Clients may signal the need for this shift by asking the therapist about possible actions for bringing about change, or the therapist may test the water by asking transitional questions like the following:

- What do you make of this? What are you thinking you'll do about this?

- Where does this leave you in terms of your drug use? What are your plans?

- I wonder what you're thinking about your drug use at this point?

- Now that you're this far, I wonder what you might do about these concerns?

The therapist's goal is to obtain some ideas about, and ultimately, a specific plan for change. It is not the therapist's task to determine how the client will change or even to teach specific skills for doing so. The essential message remains, "Only you can change your drug use, and its up to you." Additional questions may be helpful to the client in specifying a plan:

- How do you think you can accomplish that?

- What kinds of things do you think might help?

- Can you be more specific in helping me understand specifically how you intend to do that?

COMMUNICATING CHOICES
Throughout motivational interviewing, the client's autonomy, responsibility, and freedom of choice are stressed. As the client moves toward specifying plans for change, it is a good idea to emphasize these

basic realities:

- It's up to you what you do about it.

- No one can decide for you.

- No one can change your drug use for you. Only you can do it.

- You are perfectly free to go on using drugs as you were, or you can change.

EXPLORING THE CONSEQUENCES OF ACTION AND INACTION

In moving toward a specific change plan, it is helpful for clients to have a clear notion of the consequences that follow upon changing or not changing a specific behavior. Therapists can directly ask clients what they imagine the benefits and liabilities might be if they changed their drug-using behavior or if they did not change it. It is also a good idea to discuss any fears they may have about changing drug-using behavior. Questions include:

- How do you think your life might be different, both positively and negatively, if you were to stop using drugs?

- Given your past experience, what do you anticipate you are likely to experience over the next five years if you continue to use drugs as you have?

- What do you see as the advantages of changing your drug using behavior and what do you see as the advantages of continuing to use drugs as you have been?

As a follow-up to such questions, the therapist should use reflection, summarizing, and reframing. It is also possible to make a decisional balance worksheet, which lists the positives of a specific decision on one side of the page and the negatives on the other.

INFORMATION AND ADVICE

It is not unusual for clients to ask for information and advice as they move toward specific change plans. After all, if they have never attempted to change their drug using behavior, there is really no reason why they should know everything there is to know about going about it. It is appropriate for the therapist to respond to a specific request for information and advice but to do so with certain qualifications and the permission for the client to disagree. This may seem strange to some therapists, but such caution in giving information and advice leaves it clear that the client is the one who must accept and act on whatever input the therapist has to offer. It is impossible to list all the possible situations in which a client might ask for information or advice, but some general examples of the framing of responses follow:

- If you want my opinion, I can certainly give it to you. But it is important that you realize that you are the one who has to make up your own mind.

- I can tell you what I might do in a similar situation, and I'll be glad to do that, but remember that it's your choice. Are you sure you want my opinion?

- I can give you the information you are asking for, but remember that you are the one who has to decide what to do with it.

- I really can't tell you what to do in this situation, but I can share with you what I have seen other people do that has been helpful to them.

- It seems there are at least three things that might be of value to consider in your current situation. I've known other clients who have found these things helpful. But remember you have to decide what is most likely to be helpful in your case.

When asked to give an overall opinion about the client's situation, the therapist should be honest. Within the framework already suggested, the therapist can honestly address general issues.

- Since you asked, I can give you my opinion. Remember, however, that you can accept it or reject it. It's my experience that individuals I've worked with over the years who have experience similar to yours do best if they consider not using any drugs or drinking at all.

- The best advise I can give you is that it's my experience that people who want to change their drug using behavior have a lot easier time of it if they also change what they do for recreation and who they spend time with. Do you think that makes sense in your situation?

When it comes to specific advice, therapists who use motivational interviewing should be very reluctant. Clients are likely to take such advice as a prescription without accepting any real responsibility for the outcome. In such a case, even very good specific advice may be less likely to have a positive outcome. The energy that fuels behavioral change must come from the client, and that energy is largely determined by how clearly the client owns the specific means of bringing about that change. Requests for specific "how-to" advice need to be directed back to the client.

- How do you think you might best deal with that?

- You'd have to be pretty creative (or determined, or courageous, or strong, etc.) to deal with that. I wonder how you could do it.

If the client asks for specific information as opposed to specific advice, the therapist can give it. If you don't know the specific information being requested, be honest in admitting that you don't know and offer to find out by the next session or to call the client with the information as soon as you can get it. Therapists should not feel obliged to know every possible piece of information. Being an educated and competent professional often means knowing how to find out what you need to know.

EMPHASIZING ABSTINENCE
Every drug-using client should be given, at some appropriate point, a rationale for abstinence. In this way, working with drug using clients is different from working with clients who use alcohol only. Ethically, therapists are not free to encourage their clients in doing something that is actually or

potentially harmful. Since using drugs is illegal, encouraging or supporting clients in using drugs moderately leaves them open to legal harm. It doesn't matter to therapists how irrational differential laws for alcohol and drugs may be. However, in motivational interviewing, and probably in reality as well, therapists do not "permit," "let," or "allow" clients to make choices about their drug use. The choice is always the client's. In emphasizing abstinence, the following points are helpful:

- Abstinence is always safe. If you don't use any drugs you will not have any further problems with them or any further problems that arise from the use of drugs. This does not mean that you might not have other problems that may be the result of adjusting to life without drugs.

- There are a number of good reasons to experience abstinence. Among the reasons are: to find out what it feels like to live drug free, to explore more objectively one's involvement with drugs, to try out some new behaviors, to change some old habits, to make spouses happy, to keep the probation officer away, etc.

- Abstinence from drugs avoids the harm that drugs can do to the tissues of the body and allows time for healing to occur.

In emphasizing abstinence, therapists should always make it clear that it is the client's choice.

FORMALIZING A PLAN OF CHANGE

As clients move toward specifying not only what changes need to be made but also how these changes are to be accomplished, therapists need to help clients in formalizing the process. The ultimate success of any plan of change has to do with how specific and how complete it is. The object here is not to become minutely compulsive in specifying every possible element in a change process. Rather, it is to assist the client in having specified certain critical elements of the plan for change. The therapist prompting the client to explore these critical elements of the plan can do this. Possible ways to address each of these elements are:

- I wonder if you can describe for me what changes you have decided to make.

  Therapists should encourage clients to express these in positive terms (wanting to increase, improve, begin) rather than in negative (to stop, avoid, or decrease) terms.

- Would you be willing to walk me through your plan of change one step at a time? What do you intend to do first, second, etc.?

  Clients need to be encouraged to be as concrete as possible in thinking through the steps necessary to accomplish a specific behavioral change. In responding to this element of the plan, clients may request some advice and information from therapists. What has already been said about this applies here as well.

- Can you describe for me how other people can be of assistance to you in carrying out your plan of change?

Clients need to be encouraged to use the healing relationships that are or can be part of their lives. They also need to be encouraged to be very specific in how they intend to access the assistance of others.

- How will you know that your plan is working?

  Clients need to specify what they expect to see happen as a result of the proposed change. Therapists need to assist clients in being realistic about their expectations and their time frames.

- Is there anything that might interfere with your plans for change?

  Therapists can help clients anticipate possible problems that may arise as they attempt to change. Therapists can also help clients formulate plans for overcoming obstacles or developing fallback plans.

REVIEWING

As a client moves toward a specific change plan and acts on that plan, the therapist should review the client's progress. Clients can become narrowly focused on a present problem and "block out" what has already been accomplished. Likewise, as clients implement their plans, they may discover that change may be slower or require more effort than they had expected. When the therapist reviews the client's progress and reminds the client of all the reasons for change, the client can regain perspective and renew a sense of self-efficacy. It is important that the therapist use the client's own self-motivating statements.

ASKING FOR COMMITMENT

After a client has developed a plan, the therapist should ask for a specific commitment to that plan. This plan may be formalized in a behavioral contract. The contract is a formalized commitment to make changes. Usually it is best to ask for a verbal commitment and then develop the written contract with the client.

Using Motivational Interviewing with This Manual

During this phase of SBORT, therapists work with clients to explore their experience with drug use and their biopsychosocial history and functioning. The evaluation format, which follows this section, is a guide to exploring various areas of client functioning. The strategies described in the preceding section of this manual should be used to assist the client in recognizing that changes are necessary. The ideal end of this process is that clients make a specific commitment to follow through with treatment to accomplish change. This can be called engagement. Kentucky data indicate that about one third of clients who seek treatment, stay in treatment beyond the first visit. Concern about client engagement is why motivational interviewing is emphasized at the beginning of this treatment protocol.

Therapists should be familiar with the range of skills, particularly using open-ended questions and summarizing feedback, that are a part of motivational interviewing described in this manual. These two techniques are essential for the Phase I assessment and are most often needed in case management and in groups. Using open-ended questions allows the client to set the agenda and retain responsibility for change. Summarizing feedback allows the therapist to focus the client's attention to the change process.

Motivational interviewing continues to be used with case management. It is used to identify issues or problems that may be obstacles to treatment or to the behavioral goals. The emphasis may more often be on problem drug use. The same strategies that pertain to motivational interviewing in Phase I also apply during assessment.

Pretreatment and Assessment

A client assessment that incorporates motivational interviewing, (Miller & Rollnick, 1991), is an important part of therapy. With this approach, a therapist obtains both objective and subjective client information. In addition, the client obtains a clearer understanding of the need for change and can make a more solid commitment to a specific plan of change.

In most clinical settings there is a need to obtain demographic and screening information so that an appropriate disposition can be made to open each case. The therapist's attitude about assessment is related to the client's responsiveness. If a therapist believes this is valuable for meeting client's needs, the client will find the assessment process less burdensome. It is usually important for the therapist to make the purpose of the assessment clear with introductions like:

> "(Client's Name), before we can talk in a more relaxed way about what brings you here today, there is some basic information about you and your situation that I need to gather. This information is necessary for opening a counseling record, measuring the nature and extent of your situation, and establishing you as a client. It is also very helpful to me, since it allows me to get an overview of your experience and it will be valuable for counseling. Without a good evaluation, I would be of no more value to you than a blindfolded surgeon. I apologize for all the direct questions and assure you that as soon as we have finished with this part of your evaluation, we will talk in a more informal way about your experience and your concerns."

In some situations support staff can obtain demographic information. However, we recommend that qualified clinical staff obtain personal information. In this situation, the same opening remarks can be used with changes. In either case, once the introduction is completed, screening should proceed in a friendly but businesslike manner. In our experience, clients do not mind structured evaluations; as a matter of fact, they expect and respect it. It is more likely that therapists will have difficulty with this kind of information gathering. The therapist needs to make a mental note of specific information in the initial screening so that it can be explored and clarified in subsequent parts of the assessment. If someone other than the therapist collects the information, the therapist should take time to review the information confidentially before meeting the client.

Once the initial data is obtained, the tone of the interaction should change markedly. The pace should become slower and more relaxed. The therapist should adopt the attitude of an active listener. It is important to note that the assessment evaluation being presented here is a careful balance between attempting to understand the objective situation of the client and assessing his subjective interpretation of that experience. At this initial stage, a client will be either in the precontemplation or the contemplation stage of the change cycle (Prochaska and DiClemente, 1982), which is the client's perception of his experience.

A series of open-ended questions appropriate for an assessment interview using motivational interviewing techniques is provided below. The questions are sequenced in categories that are slightly different from those usually used. Based on our experience, this sequencing is closer to the way most individuals perceive and organize their experiences. The questions are not an exhaustive listing. Therapists should frame additional questions in the same open-ended format.

It is appropriate to take notes during the assessment process. In fact, we suggest that the therapist explain what is taking place: "To make sure I have an accurate picture of the your situation." The way the therapist records the information is not an issue here. Whether the therapist uses a narrative format or a checklist, this open-ended motivational format for data gathering can be used. We strongly recommend that in recording data from an assessment, therapists limit themselves to behavioral descriptions of what the client actually said and refrain from interpretations or elaboration. It is better to say, "The client talked about his belief that people were watching him and laughing behind his back" than to say, "The client has paranoid delusions." The assessment does not have to be completed in one session. As a matter of fact, we suggest that it be spread out over at least two sessions and possibly three.

At the end of each of the following sections, we recommend that the therapist summarize what the client has said. This summary offers the opportunity for the therapist to make sure the information is correctly understood and for the therapist to express empathy and reflective listening. This summarization also provides a chance to give feedback that can allow clients to change their perspective on their alcohol/drug use and its relationship to the problems of their lives. In our experience, these assessment transitions allow opportunity for applying the principals of motivational interviewing.

Assessment Questions

1. CIRCUMSTANCES LEADING TO TREATMENT

"Tell me what kind of things led up to your coming here today."

"In what ways do you think I can be of greatest assistance to you?"

If the client is seeking treatment under coercion, this is a good time, if appropriate, to disassociate yourself from the coercive forces, making it clear that your concern is the client's welfare and that the reason someone seeks treatment is not nearly so important as what happens once they get there.

2. ALCOHOL USE

"Tell me about your use of alcohol."

"What was your early experience with alcohol like?"

"What happened next?"

"What has your most recent experience with alcohol been like?"

Summarize what the client has told you; point out any discrepancy between quantity and frequency of responses given during screening and those given here. Accurately reflect changes that have occurred over time, like the increase of consumption or changes from undistilled to distilled spirits. Take time to allow the client to come to terms with the amount of alcohol consumed and the frequency of consumption. Many individuals are relatively oblivious to exactly how much and how often they drink until someone asks directly.

3. DRUG USE

"Tell me about your use of drugs other than alcohol."

"What was your early experience with (name specific drug) like?"

"What happened next with (name specific drug)?"

"What has your most recent experience with (name specific drug) been like?"

Summarize what the client has told you. Point out any discrepancies between answers given during screening and those given here. Take time to reflect an accurate picture of the drugs used; their quantity and frequency of use. As with alcohol, many individuals have only a vague awareness of how much they are using and how often. Accurately reflect changes in patterns of use occurring over time: changes in the types of drugs used, the drug combinations, the means of obtaining drugs, and other factors.

4. LIFE PROBLEMS

"What do you see as the biggest problems in your life right now?"

Review various areas of functioning: interpersonal relationships, like those with spouse, children, parents, and friends; employment and economic circumstances; legal difficulties; health and emotional problems.

"Do you see these problems related to your use of alcohol or drugs?"

"Tell me about the history of these problems."

"Tell me about the kinds of things you have done in attempting to solve these problems."

Summarize the nature and extent of the client's perceived problems. This summary provides an opportunity to link some of them to use of alcohol or drugs. Remember, however, this is not a debate! You want to raise the client's awareness that at least the possibility exists that some of these problems would not have arisen without drinking or drug use. Here, as in all other areas, support any statements that the client makes recognizing a connection between painful experience and the use of chemicals and any statement that moves toward a determination to solve problems through positive change.

5. DEPENDENCY

You may already have a good deal of information about how a dependency syndrome is presented in the life of the individual you are assessing. This information may be in the triage data in initial screening or from earlier sections of this assessment. The diagnostic criteria from the DSM-IV are listed below with appropriate questions. If you already have information on the specific criteria, it is not necessary to use the questions; simply summarize the information you already have and reflect this back to the client. Remember, three criteria are necessary for a dependence diagnosis. Not all individuals display symptoms in all criteria.

- Tolerance as defined either by the need for increased amounts of the substance to achieve a desired effect or markedly decreased effect with continued use of the same amount of the substance.

  "Do you find that you use more (name specific substance) now than in the past?"

  "Was there a time in the course of your use of (name the substance) when you used more than you did when you started?"

- Withdrawal as manifested by the characteristic withdrawal syndrome for the substance(s) taken or the same or similar substance taken to relieve withdrawal symptoms.

  "Has there ever been a time in your life when you stopped using (name the substance) and other drugs or attempted to cut back on your use of (name the drug) and other drugs? If there was, tell me about what you experienced when you did that."

  "Have you ever used drugs as a way of making yourself feel better after a bout of heavy use, like drinking to relieve a bad hangover?"

- The substance is taken in larger amounts or over a longer period of time than intended.

  "Do you ever use more of a drug than you intend to use or continue using longer than you mean to? If so, tell me about some of those experiences."

- There is a persistent desire and/or unsuccessful attempts to limit or cut down the use of the substance.

  "Have you ever made promises to yourself or to someone else about changing your use of (name the substance) and found that you were unable to keep those promises for any length of time? If so, please tell me about some of those experiences."

- A great deal of time is spent in the effort to obtain the substance, use the substance, or recover from its effects.

  "Do you have any sense that your use of (name the substance) has made it difficult for you to carry out your responsibilities at home or on the job (at school)? If so, tell me about some of those experiences."

- Important social, occupational, or recreational activities are given up or reduced because of substance use.

"Have you ever felt bad or has anyone ever criticized you because there were responsibilities to yourself or others that you could not consistently meet because of your use of (name the substance)? If so, please tell me about those experiences."

- The substance use continues despite knowledge of having a persistent or recurrent physical or emotional problem that is likely to be caused or worsened by substance use?

"Have you ever felt or has someone else expressed concern that your use of (name the substance) was causing or worsening problems with your physical or mental health? If so, please tell me about those experiences."

Now is a good time to summarize what the client has told you in a way that links the use of drugs and various problems in his life. It is also valuable to raise questions about how many problems would be eliminated or become more manageable with abstinence and recovery. Again, remember that the object is not debate. Remember that the individual may be struggling with perfectly natural ambivalence. Respect and empathize with that struggle while moving the balance in favor of abstinence and recovery. If too much resistance begins to surface, back off and continue the evaluation.

6. FUNCTIONAL ANALYSIS

This section focuses on the "function" or "use" of chemicals in the life of a client. There are two things you want to find out: (1) What events tend to precede the use of drugs and (2) What effects tend to follow the use of drugs, or what events does the client hope will follow the use of drugs? This information is often not collected in assessments and is vital for effective treatment planning especially using a social skills training approach. Start with the following questions:

"Tell me about the kinds of situations (persons and places) or ways of thinking or feeling (anxiety, sadness, boredom, and pain) that you usually experience before you start using (name the substance)."

"Tell me about the kinds of things that you usually experience when you start using (name of substance)."

"In general, does drug use do for you what you hope it will do for you?"

Some gentle probing may be necessary here. In some cases, the drug use is quite effective in the short run at resolving painful feelings, and clients will be quite aware of this effect. Often, though, in the long run, drug use will worsen the very problems that the user hopes to resolve. With a moderate amount of therapeutic skill, you can assist the client to come to this realization on his own. Also, it may be necessary to reassure the client that there are other, more effective ways to deal with various interpersonal and intrapersonal problems than using drugs and that he has the ability to learn and use these skills.

7. PERSONAL HISTORY

This part of the evaluation covers developmental, educational, vocational, legal, and marital history. The open-ended questions are designed to open the doors to these various areas, but it is important for therapists to probe a bit for specific information. Be careful not to fall into the interrogation trap where you ask questions to which the client answers in one or two words.

"Tell me what it was like growing up in your family."

"What kind of person was your mother?"

"What kind of person was your father?"

"Were there other people who were important for you as you were growing up? Tell me about them."

"Tell me about any other people in your family (grandparents, aunts, uncles, cousins, brothers, and sisters) who had or have any problems with alcohol or drugs."

"Are you aware of anyone in your family who had difficulty with depression or other emotional problems or who had an especially violent temper?"

Check for physical, emotional, and sexual abuse. Try to get an understanding of the role alcohol/drugs or mental and behavioral problems may have played in the family of origin.

"Tell me about what your experiences were like while you were in school."

"Were there specific things you were good at?"

"Were there things that caused you problems?"

Explore the possibility of learning disorders especially attention deficit disorder, with or without hyperactivity. Get a sense of whether there were any unusual problems with truancy or behavior. If school problems developed in adolescence, see if they coincide with onset of alcohol or drug use.

"Tell me about the jobs you have worked at during your life."

"If you were ever in the military, tell me about your experience there."

Listen for indications that alcohol or drug use started or worsened while the client was in military service. If the client saw combat, gently probe to see if post-traumatic stress might be present.

"Of the jobs you have worked, which one did you like best and why?"

In general, see whether at least some jobs were not lost due to the use of alcohol or other drugs. If so, reflect this connection back to the client.

"Tell me about any legal problems you have had in your life."

Probe to get a history of legal problems, if there is one. Take special note of a history of juvenile crime, especially violence. This may relate to "B-Cluster" personality disorder. Note whether the criminal behavior preceded or followed the use of alcohol or drugs. Also try to get a sense of whether any criminal behavior is the result of alcohol/drug use or whether the alcohol/drug use enhances the pleasure the client takes in criminal behavior.

"If you are currently married, tell me about your relationship with your spouse."

"If you are currently divorced, tell me about your relationship with your former spouse(s)."

"If you have children, tell me about them and about your past and present relationship with them."

See if you can understand whether present or past marital relationships encouraged substance use or were damaged by it. Also, gently probe to see how use of alcohol/drugs has affected parent-child relationships. This can be especially significant if the client's own relationship with a parent was damaged by the parent's use of alcohol/drugs. Carefully reflect the information back to the client with the alcohol/drug connection clearly implied.

8. MENTAL STATUS

Most items in this section are completed by the therapist as impressions about the client are gained throughout the interview. The items that are questions or tasks presented to the client are indicated in bold type and are listed first in this format. It is usually best to introduce these by explaining that you are going to ask the client to do things that may seem strange or irrelevant. These tasks are designed to help you understand how the client's brain is functioning and are important as part of the overall assessment. Each part is titled to indicate the dimension of mental functioning being assessed.

Concentration:
    "Would you count backward from 21 by 7s (21, 14, 7, 0)?"

If the client has too much difficulty, then:

    "Would you count backward from 21 by 3s (21, 18, 15, 12, 9, 6, 3, 0)?"

If the client finds the first task very easy, then:

    "Would you count backward from 100 by 7s (100, 93, 86, 79, 72, 65)?"

Note which task(s) the client attempted, whether it was done easily or with difficulty, whether it was done correctly or with mistakes.

Comprehension and Insight:

This next task gives the client some common sayings or proverbs and asks their meaning. Since proverbs are metaphorical expressions, it requires the ability to abstract and see similarities in order to understand their meaning. If the client stays on the literal level and is unable to generalize beyond the concrete and specific, then comprehension is concrete and insight is minimal. If the client is able to apply the "saying" to human experience, then comprehension and abstraction are good and the ability to form insight is also intact. Lengthy use of various drugs tends to affect both these capabilities, as does a lack of education and exposure to literature.

> "Would you tell me what you understand to be the meaning of this proverb or saying: 'A rolling stone gathers no moss.'"

If the individual says that moving around makes it difficult to developing any lasting attachments or relationships, or something to that effect, use the next more difficult proverb. If the individual stays on a literal level, do not go to the next proverb. Note that comprehension and insight are poor.

> "Would you tell me what you understand to be the meaning of this proverb or saying: "People in glass houses should not throw stones."

If the individual says that you should not criticize others if you have faults yourself or something to that effect, use the last proverb. If the individual stays on a literal level, do not go to the next proverb. Note that comprehension and insight are poor.

> "Would you tell me what you understand to be the meaning of this proverb or saying: "A stitch in time, saves nine."

If the individual says that taking action promptly when a problem arises can solve it with much less effort than waiting until it worsens and requires much more effort, or something to that effect, comprehension and insight are not only intact, they are quite extraordinary.

Make note if the client's understanding is concrete and lacking insight or whether comprehension is normal and the individual is capable of insight.

Judgment:
In this element you are attempting to measure how the client's ability to form appropriate judgments is functioning. You will give the client two situations that require him to make a decision and see if he is capable of making a good one.

> " I would ask you to imagine that you are in a crowded movie theater and you are the only one to smell smoke. What would you do?"

If the client says he would seek out someone in charge and inform that person, judgment is good. If the client says he would shout "Fire!" or get out of the theater without telling anyone, judgment is poor.

> "I would ask you to imagine that you are walking down the street and you find a letter, addressed and stamped which someone has dropped. What would you do with it?"

If the client says he would pick it up and drop it in the next mailbox, judgment is good. If the client says he would ignore it or attempt to deliver it personally, judgment is poor.

Memory:

There are two kinds of memory that are assessed: short-term memory and long-term memory. Usually, by this point in an evaluation you have a fairly good idea about how good a client's memory is. However, it does not hurt to use the following simple questions as a check on your perception.

"Can you tell me your mother's maiden name? Can you tell me where your father was born?"

Such questions give an indication of whether long-term memory is intact.

"Do you recall what you had for dinner last night? Do you recall the time of your last appointment with me?"

Such questions give an indication of whether short-term memory is intact.

Note the status of both short-term and long-term memory.

Orientation:

This part of mental status measures whether the person knows who he is, where he is, and when he is. Orientation is usually intact except in cases of severe impairment caused by very serious emotional disturbance or by severe organic problems in brain function. Usually by this point in assessment, it is clear whether the person is oriented. Just in case you should ever need to check it out, the following are obvious questions:

" Could you tell me your name? Where are you right now? What is the year, the month, the date?"

Note whether the individual is oriented as to person, place, and time.

Appearance:

This is a statement about the client's dress, grooming, and personal hygiene. These things are largely situational, and what is appropriate in one set of circumstances may not be in another. A client who is an auto mechanic, coming for an appointment during working hours, may be appropriately dressed and groomed if he has taken time to wash his hands even though his clothes are greasy and he is a bit disheveled. However, an accountant coming to see you in the same circumstances whose clothes are greasy and who is disheveled might be quite inappropriately dressed and groomed. Dress and grooming can also indicate a state of mind. Individuals who are depressed or who have very poor self-esteem will often be careless about the condition of their clothing and their grooming. Dress and grooming can also be a statement of attitude and belief, like the outrageous dress and grooming of a punk rocker or the shaved head of a skinhead. Comment on your impression of the client's dress, grooming, and personal hygiene using concrete and objective terms. Reserve interpretation for later.

Motor Activity:
This is a concrete description of the client's physical activity: posture, movements, and gestures. Is the client upright or slouched, still or restless, relaxed or nervous? This is also where you should comment on whether the client displayed any gross or fine tremor.

Attitude:
This is a comment on your perception of the client's attitude toward treatment and toward you. It is a spectrum that runs from cooperative and friendly to openly hostile and argumentative.

Speech:
This is where you comment on your observations about the client's flow of speech. Did the client talk a good deal or say little? Was the client's vocabulary large or restricted? Could the client make himself understood easily or did he have difficulty expressing things? Did the client answer directly and to the point or did he talk around the issue (circumstantial) or never answer at all (tangential)? Was the speech rapid or slow, fluid or halting? Were the client's statements well-organized or disorganized? Comment on all of the above.

Mood and Affect:
This is a comment on the general mood and emotional quality of the client during your time with him as indicated by what the client said and how he said it. Mood is a generalized state of feeling like sadness, happiness, and guardedness. Affect is a more specific tone of expression that we sense in voice quality and body language, as well as the content of what someone says. Both mood and affect are situational and therapists need to comment on whether the mood and affect were appropriate to the subject of the interaction.

Perception:
This is an assessment about the client's perception of self and of the world. In general, unless there is good reason to doubt the soundness of a client's perception, most addicted individuals will be normal. However, if the client expresses a sense that he is enclosed in a bubble or that things are not real (derealization), or that he is somehow not himself or is distorted in some way (depersonalization), or that he is experiencing things that others do not perceive (hallucination), then further investigation is warranted. These experiences can indicate drug effect, especially with hallucinogens or an underlying mental disorder.

Usually recording of these comments takes place between sessions with the client rather than in the client's presence. The content of the Mental Status Evaluation will be discussed with the client together with other items in the evaluation once it is completed.

9. SPIRITUAL ASSESSMENT
This is an area where many addicted individuals feel a great sense of discrepancy between what they think and believe and how they act. The object here is to engage the client in a discussion about his sense of the value, meaning, and purpose of his existence. It is not specifically a religious issue, but many clients define it in religious terms. It is also an area of discussion that people seldom broach in everyday interaction, and some clients, as well as some therapists, will feel uncomfortable and unfamiliar with

even thinking in such terms. Be patient and encourage the client to explore his beliefs. The following are some suggested open-ended questions.

"Could you tell me what you feel are the most important and valuable things in your life right now?"

"Do you have a sense that your life has a meaning or a purpose; that there is some reason why you have survived to this point?"

"How do you feel it is best for people to relate to and treat one another?"

"Do you have any sense that you are part of something that is bigger or greater than just yourself and your own needs?"

"Do you think that your actions in the past have matched your beliefs about what is important and how people should treat each other?"

"Have you ever had any regular contact with an organized religion, like a specific church? Tell me about it."

"Tell me about your best experience with that religious group."

"Tell me about your worst experience with that religious group."

"Have you ever had a special experience that you might call a 'religious' or 'spiritual' experience? If you have, would you be willing to tell me about it?"

Note whether the client has a sense of meaning and purpose to his life that goes beyond his immediate needs. Also make note of any relationships that the client gives special significance to in this regard, either with a person or an organization, and whether the experience was good or bad. Note whether or not the client has any spiritual aspirations that can only be met if he recovers. Also note if the client has none of the above. This is valuable information and may indicate the presence of developmental problems that may seriously interfere with the ability to benefit from treatment.

10. ASSESSMENT OF RISK
This element of assessment attempts to get an understanding of the probability that the client might pose a danger to himself or others. There is no way to accurately predict such risk. However, the more risk factors present, the greater the probability of harmful behavior. Suicidal risk factors are: past suicidal thoughts and attempts, present suicidal thoughts and plans, and predisposing factors (family history of suicide, depression, schizophrenia, recent losses, social isolation, loneliness, and personality disorder). Some obvious questions follow:

"Have you ever thought about harming yourself? Have you ever harmed yourself physically?"

"Have you recently had any thoughts about harming yourself or thought about how you might harm yourself physically?"

"Has anyone in your family ever taken his/her own life?"

"Do you frequently feel lonely, sad, or depressed?"

"Are there things you have lost recently that you feel very badly about?"

Harm to others attempts to assess the probability of violent behavior toward others. Factors that need to be assessed are as follows: past history of violent behavior, present thoughts or urges to harm others, use of threats of violence toward others, possession and/or fascination with weapons (with rural clients, possession of firearms or interest in firearms suitable for hunting is normal and should not be a matter of concern unless there are other risk factors present), strong persistent feelings of animosity toward specific groups of individuals or toward specific individuals.

"Have you ever hit or injured anyone? Do you often think about doing harm to get even with anyone? Is there any one person or any group of people who you feel the world would be better off without?"

Risk of victimization is an attempt to get some sense of whether or not a client is at risk of being abused. This is more important for female than for male clients. Risk factors include past history of physical or sexual abuse, and present involvement in an abusive relationship.

"Have you ever been hit, slapped, or beaten?"

"Have you ever been touched in ways that you did not want to be touched?"

"Do you currently have any contact with anyone who has harmed you or used you sexually in the past?"

Make note of all three areas of risk indicating whatever factors are involved and your assessment of the potential for harm in each.

11. BIOMEDICAL EVALUATION

Using a medical history checklist is recommended. (See the following pages.) Most treatment organizations have a medical checklist that is a required part of the initial assessment. If not, you can ask the client to fill it out prior to the motivational interview. It can be a self-report for clients who are literate, or it can be administered by the clinician.

The therapist should review a medical history, and anything that is not within normal limits should be explored. In many treatment settings, a physician reviews the medical history and makes recommendations based on it. The therapist or the physician should discuss any findings that may need further exploration with the client. Medical problems that have their origin in substance use or that are worsened by substance use should be noted and included in the "Personal Feedback" given to the client at the end of the motivational interview. Therapists should note that medical symptoms related to substance use could often be very helpful in impressing the client with a need to consider behavioral change. This is especially true for clients who are concrete in their thinking.

12. MOTIVATIONAL ASSESSMENT

When assessing motivation, it changes. In this part of the motivational interview, ask the client to list all the reasons that indicate a need for change in the alcohol/drug use behavior and all the reasons that indicate that it should stay the same. The client will probably never have looked at this issue in this way. It is also a good indicator of how much discrepancy you have raised during the assessment. The simplest method is probably also the best. Simply divide a piece of paper in half and ask the client to make a list of all the reasons for change on one side and all the reasons to continue without change on the other. You can do the actual writing or the client can. In either case, once you and the client are both satisfied that it is a fairly complete list, discuss each of the items both pro and con to get a sense of the "weight" of each. When you finish, ask the client directly what he wants to do. If the client says that he wants to continue to drink and/or use drugs as he has been, ask for one final session to review the findings of the evaluation and make it clear that he is free to do so without pressure from you. If a client decides that change would be in order, set a time to review the findings of the evaluation and to discuss specific treatment options.

13. PERSONALIZED FEEDBACK

This is the final session in the assessment process. During this session give your honest feedback to the client about what you have found in each element of the evaluation. Take care to explain why you feel each item you discuss is significant. At the same time, do nothing to induce a defensive or closed posture in the client. It is helpful to preface your remarks with statements that make it clear that the client is free to do as he pleases with the information. Such phrases are:

"I don't know what you will make of this result, but . . ."

"This may or may not be a matter of concern for you . . ."

"I don't know if this will matter to you, but . . ."

Throughout the feedback process solicit the client's reactions by such questions as:

"What do you make of this?"

"Is this what you expected?"

"I'm giving you a lot of information. I was wondering how you feel about what you have heard so far?"

Be aware of the client's body language. Frowns, sighs, a shaking head, a low whistle, or a raised eyebrow are all forms of response. Interpret them reflectively in such phrases as:

"This really took you by surprise—it wasn't what you expected."

"Looks like this is a little hard for you to hear."

"I imagine that this is a little scary."

"This must be a bit disturbing or confusing for you."

At the end of the feedback session do the following things:

1. Summarize the risks and problems that have emerged from the evaluation.

2. Summarize the client's response to the process of the evaluation including any self-motivational statements that the client has made.

3. Invite the client to correct anything that you have said in your feedback summary.

If a client chooses not to continue in treatment, wish him well and let him know that you respect his autonomy. Make sure he knows that if he should decide for treatment in the future, you would certainly welcome the decision. If the client chooses to continue in treatment, discuss the program with him and enter into a behavioral contract. Behavioral contracts are discussed in detail in the next section.

Dual Relationships

The rural clinician who practices in the region where he or she has lived for many years—or perhaps for an entire lifetime—is faced with the likelihood of having multiple role relationships with clients. In an urban setting where clinicians and clients are unlikely to meet, avoiding "dual relationships" is not difficult. The term "dual relationships" refers to the condition where the therapist and client have role relationships in addition to the clinical relationship. For example, the rural clinician's banker might seek drug and alcohol abuse treatment and turn to the clinician for assistance. In a large urban agency, the clinician would simply refer the banker to another therapist; however, in some rural settings, the clinician is the only person qualified to provide treatment. When the client is a member of the clinician's kin or friendship network, dual relationships become more complicated.

Why are dual relationships problematic? After all, one might argue that if the clinician is a close and trusted person, this will help engagement, sustain motivation, and enhance treatment. Doesn't a preexisting relationship provide a "shortcut" around the obstacles of distrust and unfamiliarity? These are reasonable questions; indeed, dual relationships present certain advantages and disadvantages that clinicians should consider.

The advantages are obvious:

- The client already knows the therapist and may establish trust more quickly.

- The client sees the therapist in other roles and has a good idea that the therapist is a decent and competent person; this expectation can increase the likelihood of successful participation in treatment.

- The client has contact with the therapist outside of the treatment setting. Such contact itself provides a "cue" for the client to recall treatment goals, and this enhances compliance.

- The therapist has a working knowledge of the client's "world" outside of treatment, and can use such objective and subjective data to develop a valid assessment and more pragmatic interventions.

- The therapist might be able to therapeutically affect the client's social network, especially if the therapist is already an influential member of that network.

However, there are disadvantages to dual relationships, which can be less obvious and might make treatment less effective:

- A preexisting relationship can make it more difficult for the clinician to maintain an objective and compassionately detached stance. This lack of objectivity can distort the assessment process and lead to ineffective treatment.

- Rural clients may be afraid of revealing negative aspects of their lives with a clinician who may also be a fellow-churchgoer or a valued customer or client. Such vulnerability might lead to loss of face or loss of business income.

- Even when the client is a *distant* blood-relative or kin by marriage, the naturally occurring pressures of family loyalty and expectations can affect the therapist. This stress can quickly erode objectivity and lead to clinical error.

- Clients may have a preexisting relationship with family members of the therapist (i.e., the clinician's sister lives on the next farm and participates in the same women's club as the client.) While such connections do not necessarily taint the treatment process, clinicians are at risk of worrying if the client's decisions in treatment (i.e., deciding to resume taking drugs) will harm the clinician's family members. This might result in the clinician trying to coerce the client to making particular decisions that will be positive for the clinician's kin network. This kind of clinician response can be very challenging to analyze and therapeutically manage.

- The clinical literature (Gutheil & Gabbard, 1993) reports that dual relationships are often the context for exploitation because of blurred professional-client boundaries. Unclear treatment frames can derail treatment. Clinicians who engage in dual relationships are at higher risk of malpractice lawsuits (Reamer, 1989), especially when financial or business ventures are involved.

- Maintaining confidentiality is already a problem for clinicians and clients living in tight-knit, rural communities. If client and clinician share the same social network, there might be more pressure on the clinician to "report" or "reassure" loved ones that the client is doing well or at least complying with treatment. Even if the clinician avoids such a breach of privileged communications, the client may live with fear that such a breach is more likely.

While it is ultimately the mutual decision of the clinician and client whether to develop or avoid a dual relationship, it is critical that both parties are aware of and prepared to manage the problems that are likely to follow. In most cases, when it is feasible, it is better to avoid dual relationships through referral to a competent colleague even if this means the clients must seek services in another county. When this is impossible, it is critical that the clinician is acutely aware of the psychosocial problems discussed above. Optimally, potential problems should be discussed with the client as well as developing a plan to address them. Clinical supervision or consultation is essential in such cases so that the therapist is not isolated when judging the impact and direction of these relationships.

Dual relationships must not include the following persons:

- All first-degree family relatives

- Persons with whom the clinician has had a preexisting, emotionally intricate relationship

- Persons with whom the clinician has ever had a sexual relationship

- Business partners, debtors, creditors or other persons to whom the clinician is connected in a significant fiduciary relationship

- Other clients as proscribed by agency policies and procedures

Risk Management

Although approaches to the special problems that therapists might face when working with rural clients are discussed in this manual, it is important to give special attention to the clinical responsibilities related to risk assessment and risk management. For this purpose, "risk" refers to the presence of factors that can lead to or significantly increase the probability of harm to a client, the therapist, or third parties affected by treatment. Risk is not always obvious. In fact, it is wise for therapists to assume that in every clinical relationship some element of risk is present. A risk assessment determines whether such risk is high, moderate, or low. Taking specific actions to deal with risk in a therapeutic manner is called risk management. Walker (1997) provides a framework for clinicians in public mental health and substance abuse treatment programs to meet the risk management and risk assessment responsibilities. Therapists can use this approach after they know their agency's policies and procedures that address risk assessment and risk management. These guidelines are based on the prevailing state and federal laws and regulations. Following these guidelines ensures compliance with statutes and regulations that mandate particular clinical responses.

Policy and procedures must be applied that can be difficult for therapists unfamiliar with risk management. Therapists can begin risk assessment by carefully conducting psychosocial assessment interviews in the pretreatment phase. A non-confrontational assessment approach increases the likelihood that a client will share what is on his mind, even if this involves admitting disturbing thoughts, feelings, and behaviors. The therapist should be open to such disclosures and avoid "punishing" or "shutting down" the client by responding in an extreme manner. Since disclosures can create anxiety for most therapists, it is possible that some therapists will "manage themselves" by attempting to rescue the client, intrusively directing the client, criticizing the client, or changing the subject to avoid disclosures. Unfortunately, these strategies can increase risk, since the client has the experience of not being heard or even being "attacked" by the therapist.

The proper interpersonal approach is concerned neutrality. This can be used with low-key body language and facial expressions, a calm voice, and sensitively paced statements and questions. Most clients will respond to this approach by talking about their concerns, even if these concerns are inherently violent or antisocial. It is crucial that therapists demonstrate empathy and provide psychological support so that clients can deal with their own anxiety. Empathy does not mean the therapist should approve or agree with the client's perceptions, behaviors, or intentions. It is very possible to support the client as a person in distress without validating plans to harm self or others, or to approve of clients' previous maladaptive behavior.

Risk assessment continues throughout treatment. In fact, clients may be more likely to disclose high or moderate risks. It is important that the therapist immediately follow up on such disclosures—usually in an individual session—to determine the level of risk and to work with the client and others to manage the risk appropriately. For example, a client discussing his anger in an anger management social skills session might reveal that he plans to harm a person who is giving him a hard time. Since discussions are often merely "all talk," there may be no intention of harming anyone. However, it is almost impossible to make that determination unless the therapist follows up and asks the client to clarify his perceptions, thoughts, feelings, and specific plans—as well as the likelihood that carrying out the aggression is actually possible. Clients often "vent" anger about persons who are no longer alive or live far away—these are low-risk situations. However, a client who is clear and specific about a planned act of violence and has access to weapons and to the potential target, presents a high-risk situation which may require hospitalization and/or contacting law enforcement as well as the potential target. Again, consultation and supervision are required to help the clinician sort out highly charged and complex clinical dilemmas.

The following examples present situations that substance-using clients might reveal to therapists. These client disclosures require risk assessment and risk management:

- Plans to harm or kill self.

- Plans to harm or kill another person.

- Is currently abusing a child, partner, or elderly person.

- Reveals that he is using substances again and feels "out of control."

- Reveals that thoughts and ideas of harming self and/or others are frequent, powerful, and/or persuasive.

- Reveals that previous self-harm or aggression was effective, pleasurable or unavoidable.

- Client does not specifically disclose the above conditions, but his statements, behaviors, or clinical presentation indicate these conditions probably exist.

When a therapist moves to risk management, he or she should have support and consultation from an agency supervisor and follow agency policies and procedures.

Clinical Supervision

Effective drug and alcohol treatment is enhanced when therapists have clinical supervision. While manual approaches like this one provide procedures for therapists, manualized treatment includes a number of potential issues that support the need for clinical supervision. Witte and Wilbur (1997: 78) identify four areas:

1. Therapists' conformity to the manual may be too "strict." In other words, therapists might prioritize manual adherence rather than actual client needs, which could lead to failure to select appropriate interventions.

2. Therapists might not adapt the treatment. In this situation, therapists use language or terms that are irrelevant or alienating for clients, which suggests minimal attention to client concerns and which results in doing treatment "to" the client.

3. On the other end of the spectrum, therapists might be "loose" in following the manual. Consequently, the approach described in the manual is neglected, leading to a "low-intensity" treatment-delivery condition.

4. Therapists can inadvertently "contaminate" the treatment with the use of techniques, language, and terms drawn from unrelated, competing, or proscribed approaches.

It is important to understand that therapists are rarely *intentional* in these actions. Because manualized approaches like SBORT are multidimensional, it takes active discipline to adhere to these interventions. At the same time it takes clinical maturity, flexibility, and acuity to tailor these interventions for specific clients and treatment groups as described in this manual. This two-pronged demand for adherence to the manual and attention to client needs can stretch the most skilled therapists. Consequently, clinical supervision can provide the psychological support and the intellectual guidance necessary to meet these challenges.

Since most drug and alcohol treatment programs have therapists with different levels of experience, skill, education, and professional development, clinical supervision—in group and individual formats—can provide varying levels of support and guidance. For example, the "novice" therapist may need more support to manage the anxiety of treating clients. On the other hand, the "seasoned" clinician may feel less need to focus on the "details" of a manualized approach because of confidence.

Personal "life" experience is also a significant factor related to how therapists adapt to a new treatment approach. A preliminary finding in our work with SBORT is the influence that "Twelve-Step" and "confrontational" approaches have on therapists who are in recovery. Therefore, it is not surprising that therapists incorporate their success with their clients and "resist" other approaches because it worked for them. Clinical supervision can be helpful in examining these and other beliefs, especially if therapists suspect other forms of treatment.

Clinical Supervision Techniques

Carroll (1998) recommends that therapist supervision using manual-driven treatment should be scheduled on a regular, predictable basis and should involve clearly defined roles, goals, and procedures that are agreed upon for both supervisors and supervisees. She also suggests that supervisor feedback should be focused and concrete to maximize comprehension and behavior change. Carroll's suggestions make sense since these principles also guide the supervisee's approach with clients.

SBORT supervision involves the following techniques that can be used and integrated into existing supervision:

Didactic approaches. Early in training and supervision, supervisors should be willing to "teach" and "demonstrate" core engagement, assessment, and treatment approaches presented. In addition, supervisors might need to introduce therapists to the theoretical concepts that underlie SBORT, so that therapists can see the connections between theory and practice. While this involves more "start-up," this understanding can help therapists tailor core interventions for specific clients without losing sight of the conceptual and technical treatment framework. This separates the "therapist" from a "technician."

Traditional supervision sessions. As therapists prepare and begin to deliver SBORT, individual and group supervision can help provide support and guidance. Sessions can include therapists "reporting" their concerns, problems, and achievements in addition to receiving supervisory feedback. We recommend that supervisors use the SBORT manual as a touchstone for such sessions, so that supervisees have the opportunity to see the manual as a tool for problem solving and as a reference that reinforces salient points outside of supervision sessions. Supervision should also address "process" issues (i.e., problems or reactions that are driven by issues outside of the content of the manual). For example, particular clients can evoke strong feelings which need to be examined in supervision so that treatment can proceed successfully. Some of these issues are addressed in a discussion of boundary problems and risk management in the manual.

In vivo and videotape observation. While this approach can initially concern therapists, there is little argument that "seeing" what the therapist is doing is superior to hearing about it. Sitting in on SBORT sessions can also give the supervisor the opportunity to observe events. This can be done unobtrusively, with participant observation and with feedback. However, we also found it useful—especially in early stages of supervision—to observe and communicate with notes or verbal consultation during session "breaks." For example, during a session on anger management a therapist became sidetracked by a group member's concerns that were only peripherally related to the social skills. When the group took a break, the supervisor suggested that the therapist might reemphasize the central points about anger management skills and take up the participant's concerns later in a case management session. This was done in an easygoing manner, which gave the impression that divergences were natural, expected, and easily corrected. Videotaping sessions and later reviews, with or without the therapist, can provide another supervision approach. The advantage of videotaping is the opportunity to examine the session and to focus supervision.

Rating scales. Rating scales are available to help with supervision. These scales can be used for structured feedback for each core treatment approach. Rating scales also neutralize arbitrary or personal irrelevant reaction.

Helping Clients Remain in Treatment to Meet Treatment Goals

In some treatment approaches, treatment planning has limited client participation. Some therapists believe that using preformatted treatment eliminates the need to involve clients in treatment planning. Structured Behavioral Outpatient Rural Therapy takes a different approach. Therapists continue to use motivational interviewing to actively engage clients in developing a client-oriented treatment plan.

Most clients who enter treatment have significant and numerous problems. Craving and the fantasy of drug use can be overwhelming. Opposition or apathy by significant others can cause clients to drop out of treatment. Economic hardships can make treatment difficult. Clients need support to stay and participate in treatment. The therapist who recognizes client problems can actively involve clients in designing practical strategies to deal with such problems to remain in treatment. Case management and behavioral contracting are two approaches that together can help clients continue in treatment and accomplish their treatment goals. While these approaches require extra time when beginning treatment, these two approaches can help avoid later problems. These approaches also help the therapist communicate in a specific way so that cognitively challenged clients can answer the question, "What am I supposed to do?"

The following sections describe case management and behavioral contracting. Two ways of planning—the *client strengths assessment* and the *behavioral contract*—are described. Each section begins with a discussion of theory and research. These sections describe case management and behavioral contracting. Since these approaches may be unfamiliar, it is important to review them. Understanding the basic principles and special issues involved with their use can help therapists become confident and flexible.

At first it might be difficult to see the link between case management and behavioral contracting. Here's one way to think about the link: Case management is an approach to help clients stay in treatment by helping them meet their basic needs—food, clothing, housing, employment, and medical care. Therefore, the therapist assesses clients' needs and helps each client develop a case management plan to meet those needs.

Once a case management plan is developed, the therapist begins to consider specific behaviors that will help the client meet substance abuse treatment goals such as "Attending three Intensive Outpatient (IOP) groups this week." Incorporating behaviors into a format called a behavioral contract helps motivate clients because clients receive rewards if they do certain things (e.g., "My wife will cook a special meal if I attend two IOP groups this week") and suffer unpleasant consequences if they do not do certain things (e.g., "Failure to attend the IOP meetings will result in therapist contacting probation officer").

The therapist can take the following steps in the planning process:

- Review the client's psychosocial assessment. Look for problems that might impede treatment participation. Also look for client strengths and resources.

- Meet with the client. Remember to encourage client participation as the plan is developed. Using the client strengths assessment form, collaborate with each client on his current needs and the possible resources that can be used to help meet those needs. Develop a case management plan.

- Discuss the main treatment goals the client wishes to accomplish, for example, "I want to abstain from all drug and alcohol use." These goals include both long-term and short-term goals, such as weekly goals versus monthly goals. A behavioral contract should be used to specify behaviors that will help accomplish those goals, target dates for those behaviors, key players who will participate in meeting these goals, and reinforcements that will motivate clients to meet those goals.

- Follow the case management plan as the client enters and participates in treatment. This approach can reduce the likelihood that the client will leave treatment because of lack of transportation and housing problems.

- Monitor the behavioral contract. Be sure client reinforcements are provided as agreed upon in the contract. This will help motivate clients to reach their treatment goals.

Case Management

Case management is an essential part of substance abuse treatment and aftercare. The term "case management" means different things to different people. For example, case management has been defined as "a method of providing services whereby the [professional] assesses the needs of the client and the client's family . . . and arranges, coordinates, monitors, evaluates, and advocates for a package of multiple services to meet the specific client's complex needs." (NASW, 1995) A common thread in the various definitions of case management is coordination to link services to individuals with the possibility of monitoring activities (Leukefeld, 1990).

These standards also emphasize interventions at micro-, mezzo-, and macro-levels; i.e., the case manager should be acting to achieve goals for the individual client, creating linkages with the resource systems and improving the nature of those systems, as well as influencing social policies that impact delivery systems (NASW, 1995).

Case management has changed since the late 1960s through the 1970s when mental health services moved from long-term, inpatient psychiatric settings to outpatient community mental health centers. Case management has a history of being developed in medical settings in which social workers or nursing staff were often responsible for patient discharge services. Case management services for mental health and, subsequently, substance abuse, were found to be useful. During the transition from inpatient to outpatient treatment, case management became popular. It has remained popular throughout the 1980s and 90s, reviving new energy from the advent of escalating inpatient costs, less reimbursement, capitated contracts, and needs for services including utilization review.

Case management is often undefined, or at best, is not standardized. The literature describes a continuum of case management models, ranging from linking clients with services, which is called "brokering," to intensive or comprehensive case management, which is often called "full-support" or "clinical" management. Clinical case management uses an approach in which many services are coordinated by, and sometimes provided by, the case manager. Other types of case management include "strengths" management, in which abilities and positive characteristics in the client, the client's support systems, and the client's community, are emphasized, and the "rehabilitation" model, where services are often provided, and skill-building, often in groups, is provided by the manager or at the sponsoring agency.

Case manager responsibilities also vary according to the type of case management. In all models, assessment is a primary responsibility. Since a case manager is frequently the entry point into services for substance abuse clients, screening and needs assessment can be a responsibility during the initial interview. This is an important point of contact for a client, who often bases further treatment decisions on this interview.

Rose and Moore's (1995) review of the literature argues that case management usually involves five basic functions:

1. Outreach to or the identification of clients

2. Assessment of needs

3. Service or treatment planning

4. Linking or referring clients to proper resources

5. Monitoring cases to ensure services are properly utilized

The case manager might be responsible for all or only several of these functions. Additionally, case managers often work in teams, which distribute these responsibilities among specialists; such a procedure is typical in many multidisciplinary team models (Panzarino & Weatherbee, 1996).

It is probably insufficient to simply list functions without discussing what kind of theoretical or methodological framework will guide the case manager as he/she enacts these functions. Some case management models specify practice frameworks. The *therapeutic model* emphasizes the case manager's responsibility to provide therapeutic services to clients. For example, Lamb (1980) argues that because mentally ill clients benefit as much from the manager-client relationship as from the actual community resources, the case manager should consciously use the relationship and other therapeutic principles to assist the client.

The *traditional broker model,* or the *coordinator-manager model* (Weissman, Epstein & Savage, 1983), focuses on the management of resources and resource providers in complex systems. Goals are primarily developed by the professional/team and the case manager coordinates preexisting resources. The case manager—through telephone contacts and meetings with resource providers—links the client with the proper mix of services. While this model seems efficient, Rubin (1992) argues that it might be simply adding layers of bureaucracy. Its assumption that adequate resources already exist is also flawed when considering locations that have few community resources (Bachrach, 1993).

The strengths perspective for case management is based on six principles (Rapp, 1992: 46):

1. The focus is on individual strengths rather than pathology.

2. The case manager—client relationship is primary and essential.

3. Interventions are based on client self-determination.

4. The community is viewed as an oasis of resources, not as an obstacle.

5. Aggressive outreach is the preferred mode of intervention.

6. People suffering from disorders can continue to learn, grow, and change.

The strengths perspective includes careful focus on the client's needs and goals. It demands an open, creative attitude on the part of the case manager—not merely a knack for reframing client problems to make them more palatable. The result should be the enhanced individuality of the client, the empowerment of the client, and the development of a working partnership between client and professional. Rapp (1992) admits that this is an extremely demanding agenda for the case manager, especially when client levels of functioning are unevenly or globally impaired.

The strengths-based case management approach has shown improved outcomes for employability, retention in treatment, and reduced drug use through retention in treatment (Siegal et al., 1995). Strengths-based case management has been used with both female (Brindis and Theldon, 1997) and male substance abusers (Siegal et al., 1995). The success of this approach rests on a valid, careful elicitation of the client's strengths in the context of her current situation and the client's desires and aspirations. Kishardt (1992: 70) has developed a format to guide the case manager and client through the client strengths assessment process. This format is presented in Figure 3.1. It focuses on factors related to Current Status, Client Desires/Aspirations, and Resources—Personal/Social in six areas: (1) Daily Living Situation, (2) Financial, (3) Vocational/Educational, (4) Social Supports, (5) Health, and (6) Leisure/Recreational Supports.

Phase I—Case Management Sessions

The case manager has a critical role to play during Part I of therapy. He or she works closely with the client to identify resources and unmet basic human needs as well as areas that can impact client participation in treatment. For example, the client might need to solve transportation problems in order to seek and maintain employment. At the same time, addressing that problem can also help the client get to therapy appointments.

The overall goals of Part I are to elicit important information about the client and to motivate the client to engage in treatment. The case manager can contribute to those Part I goals by taking the following steps:

1. Before meeting with the client, review the assessment results. Identify areas that seem to indicate significant problems for the client. If the client presents with resources, identify those as well.

2. When meeting with the client, use the motivational interviewing approach. One way to do this is to briefly review the assessment results and ask the client which areas are most important to her. Use the **Client Strengths Assessment form** (Figure 3.1) to assist the client in identifying resources and strengths. It is imperative that the case manager builds a collaborative relationship with the client. This approach forbids coercion. Remember that the role of the therapist is to help the client to become motivated to participate in the treatment.

3. After completing the strengths assessment outlined in Figure 3.1, develop a **behavioral contract** with the client (See Figure 3.2 for the outline of the contract and Figure 3.4 for a completed contract). Discussed strategies can be included in the contract. This contract should also include the basic requirements for participation in Part II of therapy (e.g., attending social skills groups), and other requirements for client participation in the program. The contract should be quite specific and consequences for completion or failure to complete made explicit. Because you will be meeting biweekly with the client in Part II, there will be ample opportunities to renegotiate and revise this contract. The more the client participates in developing strategies and choosing consequences, the more motivated the client will be to stay in treatment and participate.

Client Name _____ Case Manager_____

Date _____

CURRENT STATUS: What is going on today? What is available now?	CLIENT DESIRES ASPIRATIONS: What do I want?	RESOURCES—PERSONAL SOCIAL: What have I used in the past?
	DAILY LIVING SITUATION	
	FINANCIAL/INSURANCE	
	VOCATIONAL/EDUCATION	
	SOCIAL SUPPORTS	
	HEALTH	
	LEISURE/RECREATIONAL SUPPORTS	

WHAT ARE MY PRIORITIES?   1.   3.

                           2.   4.

CASE MANAGER COMMENTS	CLIENT COMMENTS
CASE MANAGER SIGNATURE/DATE _____	CLIENT SIGNATURE/DATE _____

Figure 3.1 *Client Strengths Assessment (Kishardt, 1992)*

4. At this point, review the **behavioral contract** with the client. Ask the client if she can think of any reason that any part of the agreement might not work. For example, if a client who does not have her own transportation "promises" to attend all sessions, you might query how she would manage transportation. If that was already covered, you might ask the client if a contingency plan exists if the original plan falls through.

Phase II—Case Management Sessions

The goals of Phase I are to understand and motivate the client. Case management during Phase II continues that process through individual sessions with the client. During this phase, clients are participating in social skills training sessions, which utilize a group process. The case management sessions are the place where the client can address individual issues.

These meetings are a significant part of SBORT because they can assist the client in completing and enhancing treatment by overcoming obstacles that typically prevent treatment completion. These are the five major goals in the Phase II case management process:

1. To help the client stay motivated to engage in treatment, and in some cases, to advance clients from lower to higher categories of motivation.

2. To help the client make specific connections between the social skills groups and her own situation.

3. To identify and address *external factors* that place the client at risk for relapse. These are the areas most typically associated with case management, i.e. "concrete" resources like housing, transportation, employment, etc.

4. To identify and address *internal factors* that place the client at risk for relapse. These include but are not limited to the following:

   • past or current trauma, e.g., family violence, criminal victimization, sexual trauma

   • co-morbid disorders such as depression, anxiety, panic, hypomania, thought disorder

   • cognitive and learning disorders (e.g. illiteracy)

   • personality traits that threaten engagement and completion such as avoidance, hostility, dependence, perfectionism, preoccupation with self.

   • family and peer influences that encourage substance misuse and impede recovery

5. To monitor and revise the behavioral contract.

The case manager works closely with the client to track compliance with the contract and to solve problems as they arise. Early proactive attention to problems can enhance the client's participation. The case manager also has an unparalleled opportunity to individually reinforce client successes. It is crucial

BEHAVIORAL CONTRACT WITH _____

DATE: _____

LONG-TERM GOAL (use a separate sheet for each long-term goal):

_____

_____

Measurable short-term goals toward achieving long-term goal	Persons Responsible	Target Date	Reward/Consequences

Client signature _____

Case Manager signature _____

Appropriate family/significant other signature _____

Figure 3.2 *Behavioral Contract*

that client successes (and approximations to success) are reinforced quickly, consistently, and as specified in the contract. Paying attention to and praising client success during individual meetings are significant reinforcers that can increase positive behaviors. Sessions are also the place where the contract is updated and modified. For example, many goals will be short-term and will need to be evaluated and revised. The case manager's intelligent negotiation with the client also offers a wonderful model of interpersonal relationship for clients.

These five goals are challenging. The following steps are presented to enable the case manager to structure the session so that the goals can be consistently addressed.

1. At the beginning of the session use the motivational interviewing approach. A good opening question is: "How are things going for you as you begin treatment?" A good question after the client has begun attending groups is: "How have you found the social skills groups over the past week?" The case manager needs to listen without criticizing and to reflect significant parts of what the client has said.

   If the client has not attended group sessions, it will be especially important to discover why that has happened and to work firmly, but non-punitively, to change that behavior. It is also important to track the client's completion of the practice exercises. Positively reinforce (e.g., praise) success, and work with the client to overcome obstacles to completion.

2. Clients may report that external factors have been sufficiently addressed so that things are going better in their lives and that they are able to participate in treatment. If a client reports otherwise, identify the unmet need and work with the client to meet it. Review the completed **Client Strengths Assessment** form in Figure 3.3. This review will help the case manager and client to recall what resources and areas of need were addressed. These might need to be revised. For example, in Part I the client might have identified transportation as a resource ("I own my own car"). However, since that time the client's car has broken down and cannot be immediately repaired. What was once a resource has now become an area of need that must be met.

   At this point you can brainstorm possible solutions or use a thought map to lay out the problem and analyze various alternatives.

3. The client might identify (or the case manager might note) internal factors that are impeding treatment or that have been triggered by treatment. The case manager will be aware of the client's assessment and history of internal factors. For example, some clients could have reported that discussion of the sources of anger in one of the social skills sessions triggered their memories of abuse, neglect, and sexual trauma. Since the group setting is not the appropriate forum for self-disclosure of previous trauma, individual sessions are the best place for the client to discuss such issues. Ongoing problems, like present victimization by a spouse or lover, might also emerge during the session.

   Some case managers might find such disclosures overwhelming and see them as topics to be avoided. This approach to therapy positions the case manager as helping the client to begin to deal with these issues. At the point of disclosure, the case manager should listen carefully and validate the client's concerns and emotions. To structure these problems, the case manager should use the thought map to identify the problem and to explore historical factors shaping the problems and various ways the client can cope in the present.

This is not intensive psychotherapy but a structured cognitive-behavioral management approach with the goal of enhancing client coping. In many cases, skills taught in group sessions can be connected to the problem at hand.

In other cases, the client may need a referral to another professional. Case managers are urged to consult with their supervisor for cases that are complex and/or require referral. The goal here is to assist the client to cope, not to change the past, reconfigure client personality, or reconstruct memories. Some clients will require medical and psychiatric consultation—especially when disorders of thought, mood, and anxiety are involved—so psychiatric and other clinical support should be used. Some internal factors may involve risk management issues. Seek supervision for such cases. Sometimes carefully coordinated care involving the case manager, group leader, and supervision team will be essential for the client to stay in treatment and to deal with internal issues.

4. Finally, review the **behavioral contract** with the client. Check to ensure the following are completed:

   - The client and case manager have reviewed the conditions from the previous week and these have been reinforced and/or addressed.

   - The goals and behaviors have been updated and revised to reflect the results of the current session. Be sure consequences have been stipulated for each behavior.

   - The client fully understands the agreement. Be sure to explore possible obstacles to successful contract execution and develop contingency plans to address obstacles.

These four steps will demand careful structuring of the session and attention to time constraints. The case manager must skillfully plan how to approach clients with an eye to completing these required steps while allowing the session to move with some flexibility and moments of spontaneity.

Client Name *John Robinson* Case Manager *Betty Jones* Date_____

CURRENT STATUS: What is going on today? What is available now?	CLIENT DESIRES/ ASPIRATIONS: What do I want?	RESOURCES—PERSONAL & SOCIAL: What have I used in the past?
Housing is O.K., but I wish I lived closer to town. Flood season is a problem. *No car right now.*	DAILY LIVING SITUATION, e.g., housing, basic needs.	*My sister and Uncle Bill have driven me to work in the past (when I was sober). They might help me to get to treatment or a new job.* *I need to look for a new place for Mary and me.*
Mary has a decent job, but money is short. I lost my last job. Someone said I need a GED.	FINANCIAL/INSURANCE	*Case manager said she would help me talk with job people to look for a job.*
I can farm and weld and work on vehicles. But I hate day labor.	VOCATIONAL/EDUCATION	*I can check again at the county high school about GED. My case manager said maybe Voc-Rehab.*
My wife, Mary the most. Sue (sister), Uncle Bill, some of my mother's people.	SOCIAL SUPPORTS	*They are real glad about my coming for help for my problem. They might help me with my parents and other kin.*
High blood pressure—real bad nerves.	HEALTH	*Take medication Dr. Combs gave me.*
I used to go hunting and fishing. *Spend time with Mary again.*	LEISURE/RECREATIONAL SUPPORTS	*Used drug and alcohol for this, but I just can't anymore. I'd like to have fun again and feel good around people.*

WHAT ARE MY PRIORITIES?   1. *Quit drugs and alcohol*   3. *Find a good job*
   2. *Attend treatment*   4. *Get back with family*

CASE MANAGER COMMENTS *John seems very committed to making changes but needs support to reach priorities. I will help with this and talk with some of his folks, too.*	CLIENT COMMENTS *I need help doing this but want to. I will work with Miss Betty.*
CASE MANAGER SIGNATURE *Betty Jones*	CLIENT SIGNATURE *John Robinson*

Figure 3.3 *Client Strengths Assessment (Adapted from Kishardt, 1992)*

Behavioral Contracting

Changing drug and alcohol use can be enhanced with a behavioral contract. A behavioral contract is a written agreement between the client and the therapist. Sometimes significant others are also part of a contract. Using a contract to establish specific therapy goals has been widely used and has important implications for treatment involvement. While these kinds of contracts are not legally binding, signing a name to an agreement often intensifies the importance of the agreement and encourages client participation (Gambrill, 1997).

Behavioral contracts have been widely used in many areas of education and therapy. For example, contracts have been found to be effective in modifying eating behavior in anorexic females (Solanto et al., 1994), and weight loss (Anderson et al., 1993). Contracting with suicidal patients to agree not to engage in harmful behaviors has been shown to be somewhat effective (Pary et al., 1988; Kernberg, 1993). Other studies report the effectiveness of contracting for establishing behavioral limits of the treatment for those with personality disorders (Yeomans et al., 1993; Miller, 1991; Selzer et al., 1990); for decreasing juvenile probationary violations (Welch & Holborn, 1988); and for increasing family involvement in reducing schizophrenic clients' recidivism (Heinssen et al., 1995; Atwood, 1990). Students have improved their attention to tasks and increased their emotional self-control (Ruth, 1996) with behavioral contracting.

Behavioral contracting increases treatment compliance (Gambrill, 1997). For example, it has been shown that using behavioral contracts with clients who are terminating treatment increased the likelihood that they attended aftercare (Singh et al., 1987). Using behavioral contracts with family members increased disulfiram (antabuse) compliance for alcohol-dependent clients (O'Farrell, 1989; O'Farrell et al., 1986). Family contracts with cocaine abusers increased positive treatment outcomes (Higgins et al., 1994) and opiate-dependent clients relapsed less often (Calsyn et al., 1994) when contracting was used. In addition, outcomes for dual diagnosis clients were enhanced when behavioral contracting was a part of treatment (Woody et al., 1984; Lineham, 1993).

An early study of cocaine abusers by Anker and Crowley (1982) examined the use of written behavioral contracts that incorporated severe consequences for failure to stay abstinent. Consequences included loss of job, loss of professional license, or disclosure of the lapse to probation/parole officers with threat of returning to jail. The use of contracts was considered successful because not one of the clients who refused to use the behavioral contract remained in treatment the entire month while those who did contract continued in treatment and remained abstinent during treatment. These results could be attributed to self-selection, since only motivated clients agreed to sign a treatment contract. Nevertheless, the study suggested that contracts can positively impact immediate treatment outcomes.

Negative reinforcement behavioral contracts have been used extensively with impaired professionals. For example, Crowley (1984) reported on seventeen drug-dependent medical professionals who gave their therapists unmailed letters addressed to their licensing board which described their drug use and surrendered their professional licenses. The patient contracted that the letter would be mailed if there were a positive urinalysis, or if the client failed to appear for scheduled monitoring. Only two professionals lost their licenses through these behavioral contracts. Professionals were given the opportunity to continue contracting over several years. When contracts were in place, recidivism remained very low. However, when contracts were not renewed, there was an increase in drug use.

Positive reinforcements are also effective in increasing compliance and abstinence with behavioral contracts. Contingency contracts in methadone settings have been used, and results indicated that when positive reinforcements were created for clients signing the contracts, more "clean" urine samples were produced over a longer time (Stizer et al., 1992; Silverman et al., 1996). The positive reinforcements included take-home methadone doses for those clients who reported to the clinic each day. The results indicated that clients with lower drug-use baselines responded best to behavioral contracting. Another effective positive reinforcer for decreasing illicit drug use and associated criminal and HIV-risk behavior included increasing methadone dosing for those who were free of other drugs (Nominal & Crowley, 1990).

Developing the Behavioral Contract

The behavioral contract is most useful as an individualized treatment plan in which the client and the clinician commit to reaching measurable goals by following a specific plan. Both the client and clinician need to commit to abiding by this plan in order for the plan to be successful. Developing such a contract in Phase I of treatment can enhance client participation in Phase II.

It has been suggested that the moment of negotiating a behavioral contract is the crucial moment in the therapeutic relationship (Selzer et al., 1990). It is important that a clinician carefully develop the contract to reflect client needs and employ effective strategies. When developing a behavioral contract, the therapist must meet structural objectives (Granvold, 1997). In other words, a contract should clearly state the problem being addressed, the reasons the problem is being addressed (the antecedents) and the areas of change. Contract elements should include:

- A clear and detailed description of assignments or expectations.

- Positive reinforcement gained if the assignment is completed.

- Consequence for failure to complete or approximate the assignment.

- Specific ways that the contracted response is to be observed, measured, or recorded.

- Immediate rewards and consequences after the completed task.

As part of this negotiation, discuss any obstacles that might interfere with the client's full participation. Help the client to find resources or solutions to anything that would pose a barrier to participation. With this discussion you are moving into the next phase of motivational interviewing, in which you will be fostering the client's sense of self-efficacy and acting as a case manager to assist the client in accessing solutions to those problems that pose a threat to treatment and recovery.

Specify in the behavioral contract exactly what the client will do over the next few weeks as well as what you or other members of the program staff will do to assist him. Keep the time frame of the contract short, no more than two weeks, with the understanding that you will be renegotiating it throughout treatment as things change. Talk about the contract in terms of a behavioral treatment plan rather than as a list of the client's obligations. The purpose of such a document is to make it very clear and very explicit what is expected of everyone in the therapeutic relationship. Also make it clear that the contract can be renegotiated at any time if it is felt that the expectations are not in the client's best interest. Therapists need to approach the behavioral contract as a serious but time-limited commitment to the client and assist the client in adopting a similar attitude.

Example Contract

Figure 3.4 is one example of a behavioral contract used for a specific weekly assignment, particularly designed for a rural client who does not have ready access to therapy and recovery groups. This client has the long-term goal of staying sober because he decided that his drug use is interfering with his relationships with his family. Identified short-term goals toward achieving the long-term goal are listed in the first column, followed by the name of the person(s) responsible for helping to carry out the goal and the dates it will be accomplished. In this example contract, free transportation to therapy and AA is given as a positive reinforcement, and paying for transportation a negative reinforcement in the case of relapse.

Special Issues

1. Short-term contracting should begin with a small number of realistic and achievable goals. Moving incrementally is important for ongoing compliance (Linehan, 1993). Contracts will probably fail if goals are unattainable, not understood, or if the client is exhibiting neurotoxicity from long-term drug or alcohol use. Therapists must avoid developing behavioral contracts that are harmful to clients. Therapists and supervisors need to frequently examine contracts for potential problems. According to Miller (1990), difficulties with formulating contracts develop when:

    *   Contracts are too restrictive or "parental."

    *   Contracts appear to be punishing or rejecting.

    *   The contract substitutes for therapy rather than enhancing therapy.

    *   The therapist is no longer vigilant in observing the contract.

    *   The therapeutic relationship is not established, or is estranged, and the contract becomes a source of resistance.

    *   The contract is too rigid, does not allow for client determination, or does not include client input.

    *   Therapist countertransference (anger, for example) is present (see also Selzer, et al., 1987).

    *   The client does not have the skills to carry out the contract (skills training should be part of the session).

    *   Contracts are too vague or do not have appropriate contingencies.

BEHAVIORAL CONTRACT WITH *JOHN ROBINSON*

DATE: _____

LONG-TERM GOAL (use a separate sheet for each long-term goal): *I want to stay off drugs & alcohol because it is getting in the way of my family relationships.*

Measurable short-term goals toward achieving long-term goal	Persons Responsible	Target Date	Reward/Consequences
Attend weekly counseling sessions.	Me My therapist My sister, Sue	1/5/98 1/10/98	Sue will drive me free. If I drink, I have to pay Sue $25 for rides to sessions.
Attend AA meetings every Sunday.	Me Uncle Bill	1/9/98 1/16/98	Bill will drive me to AA free if I stay sober. Trips will cost $25 if I drink.
Take prescription each morning and evening.	Me My wife, Mary	Daily	Mary will help me and we will work together.
Talk to wife every day about how I am doing.	Me My wife, Mary	Daily	If we agree we had a good discussion, I get to choose a "fun" activity for us next day—restaurant, go fishing, etc.
I will be on time for all group sessions.	Me Therapist	1/6/98 1/11/98 1/13/98	My therapist will report this weekly to my probation officer. Stay in program and graduate.
Attend two "check-in" appointments with my case manager.	Me Case manager	1/12/98 1/14/98	Will receive feedback on my progress and get support for my efforts. Will get help connecting to employment services.
I will continue to work on my GED review at least 30 minutes per day.	Me Case manager	Daily	If I turn in my completed study guides, I will get help signing up and taking my GED exam.

Client signature   John Robinson
Case Manager signature   Betty Jones
Appropriate family/   Mary Robinson (wife)
significant other signature   Sue Robinson (sister)

Figure 3.4 *Example of a behavioral contract for one long-term goal*

NOTE: *The strategies for positive reinforcements and negative contingencies, as well as reasons for not using substances, can also be shown on a thought map, which may be useful for developing and using behavioral contracts.*

- The client does not "buy into" the contract, although he appears willing to comply.

Several of these warnings should be particularly observed with rural clients who may not have had exposure to either a contract or therapy and may be approaching the sessions with caution. Behavioral contracting should be developed after the motivational interviewing has been completed and therapeutic rapport has been established. Therapists should also make certain that when behavioral contracting items are determined, the client has, or is learning, the skills necessary to be successful.

As clients gain control over their drug-using behavior, they begin to establish self-respect and a sense of self-mastery in recovery. Clients also begin to experience the gratification that comes from being successful and meeting goals. In addition, as a client begins to think more clearly about choices and consequences, the need for written behavioral contracts should decrease. Contracts are most useful during the period when thoughts and desires are not internalized, and the client needs additional structure. Contracts—especially those used with the client's family and social support network—can provide important and needed structure.

2. Some therapists worry that developing positive reinforcers with rural clients will be next to impossible because of the limited number of "rewards" available in non-urban communities, e.g., movies, restaurants, shopping malls, etc. Others are concerned that developing reinforcers is a form of "bribery," which will send the wrong message to the client.

First, it is important to remember that positive reinforcers are a short-term approach to increasing the frequency of targeted behaviors. Reinforcers give the client time to try new behaviors, get rewarded for his efforts, and begin to experience the pleasure of these new behaviors. If therapy is successful, the client will begin to develop the new behaviors as "habits," making external reinforcement eventually unnecessary. Reinforcers sustain the client through the difficult process of change.

Second, it is rarely necessary to dream up some super reward system for the client. In fact, the best way to develop a list of positive reinforcers is to elicit them from the client or significant other. Many therapists find that clients have simple desires that can be developed into positive reinforcers. Here is a list of positive reinforcers that clients have discussed in therapy sessions:

- Some romantic time with their partner

- More play time with their children

- Free babysitting

- A day off to go fishing or hunting

- An afternoon trip to a favorite place (e.g., a state park)

- Long-distance telephone calls to family and friends

- Rides to therapy and other activities (e.g., church, visiting family)

- A fishing rod or hunting rifle

- Low-cost housing (e.g., a room at a relative or friend's home)

- Being taught a new skill

- Receiving special assistance in a job search

- Taking classes to earn a GED

The rural therapist can explore with the client what activities and things would make his life easier and more pleasurable. If family and friends can become involved even minimally as the "delivery system" for some of these rewards, the client and therapist can develop a more varied menu of positive reinforcers.

Third, many clients are already receiving such rewards from others with no expectations for behavior change. The therapist should explicitly identify these as rewards and link continuation of these to the target behaviors in the contract. For example, one client was receiving free room and board from an aunt who was supporting her recovery process. The therapist identified "room and board" as a valuable reward that would continue to be delivered as long as the client participated in treatment. The aunt agreed to continue to provide this and other financial support for the client's children during the treatment period. While it might be true that the aunt would have done this anyway, including it in the contract allowed her generosity to be explicitly developed as a reinforcer linked to behavior change. This approach also allowed the therapist to utilize the cultural imperatives of family loyalty and assistance as an adjunct to therapy rather than to pathologize these as "enmeshment" or "codependency."

Thought Mapping

Thought mapping is a way of helping clients learn from their experiences by organizing their personal thoughts (cognition) and behaviors visually, like a road map. Substance abuse clients in early recovery frequently have problems with understanding, learning, and managing abstract notions (Grant et al., 1977; Meek et al., 1989; and Czurchry et al., 1994). Thought mapping has been an effective way of assisting clients in early recovery to overcome cognitive deficits (Knight et al., 1994). Thought mapping has been found to be effective with cocaine abusers (Joe et al., 1994), individuals with attention deficit problems (Czurchry et al., 1994), and individuals with little education (Pitre et al., 1996).

All of us store and retrieve information through relationships. Our experiences with persons, situations, and events are linked to one another through associations. This is why a new experience that is similar to an old experience can trigger a flood of memories that are linked by association. These experiences and their links form a complex map of experience that we rely on for interpreting, learning, and growing. When we attempt to communicate to another person some aspect of our own experience, we are really communicating some piece of this complex map. If the other person has experiences and an internal map that is similar to our own, that communication can take place far more easily and with less risk of misunderstanding. If, on the other hand, that person's experience is very different than our own, or if their internal map has very different links, than it becomes much more difficult to communicate and there is a much greater chance of being misunderstood.

Thought mapping focuses on internal and unconscious processes to make them external and conscious. In doing this we can help clients visually present the pathways that lead to either constructive or destructive behaviors. As clients become more aware of this process, they can assume more responsibility for their behavior, their lives, and they can make choices about how they will think, feel, decide, and behave.

The overlap of population characteristics and the population with which thought mapping is most effective—those with lower literacy, lower verbal skills, and less education—suggests that incorporating thought mapping into social skills sessions would facilitate behavior change.

Thought mapping is a way to "look at" and present information that has been used by drug abuse therapists (Czuchry et al., 1994). This approach uses nodes—boxes and ovals—to represent feelings, thoughts, and actions. Links or lines are used to visually show relationships between nodes. For this project, the clinician and the client will jointly complete a map by filling in personal concepts on the thought map.

Thought mapping helps therapists ask questions about clients' experiences, which assists in exploring their other experiences. The therapist then maps these experiences and the links between them to create a representation of the clients' thoughts and behaviors. With these maps, clients can begin to see how some experiences are related to desirable outcome while others to undesirable outcomes. This information can assist clients in seeing more clearly where changes need to take place and why these changes are likely to be helpful.

It is also possible for a therapist to interact with clients, either individually or in a group, and map the process as it unfolds. This is another approach to mapping. However, in this approach the previously described method of mapping is not used. Instead blank maps are used. A blank map is used to guide a therapeutic interaction in a specific way. When using a blank map, the therapist assists clients to complete the blanks so they can begin to gain an understanding of the specific skill. In this manual, thought mapping is used for the social skills sessions on Problem Solving, Anger Awareness and Management, and, Awareness and Management of Negative Thinking. An example of the map used in these sessions is presented as Figure 4.1.

The main purpose of thought mapping is to help clients to personally understand their cognition and behavior so that they can identify their own individual problem-solving strategies. Specifically, thought mapping is used to help: (1) problem recognition—understanding how drug use is related to other behaviors (precontemplation stage); (2) problem identification—specifically those circumstances, feelings, and values that contribute to drug use and other behaviors (contemplation stage); (3) consider various solutions—identify behavioral options available for solving problems (contemplation stage); (4) select best alternative—make a choice of action based on a rational projection of probable outcomes and their associated behaviors (action stage); and, (5) assess the effectiveness of a solution—set criteria to determine whether specific behaviors can be successfully achieved to solve a problem (action stage) (Prochaska & DiClemente, 1982).

Thought Mapping Goals
After using a thought map, clients will be able to:

1. Understand how their problems are related to substance abuse—Recognize the Problem.

2. Specify feelings, thoughts, and actions by others and self that contribute to drug use and other problems—Personalize the Problem.

3. Identify a positive behavioral option—Consider a Solution.

Using the Map
A thought map provides a personal and visual presentation to the substance abuser of how problems can lead to desirable behavioral outcomes as well as undesirable outcomes using a problem-solving approach. The map is used to help the client focus clearly on linking his actions with other actions and feelings and solution(s).

The specific steps to use in presenting thought mapping are:

*   Put a blank map on a clipboard or flip-chart and use it as the focus for discussion—Figure 4.1. (This map is modified from Dansereau et al., 1993)

*   Briefly introduce the thought mapping approach.

    NOTE: Emphasize that mapping discussions should be as straightforward as possible to focus on specific problems, identified by the client, that are related to his behavior, concentrating on one problem at a time.

- With a thought map on a flip-chart, folded in half with the top half of the map showing, begin the mapping, using the map model in Figure 4.1. Start by asking the client about the specific problem he had that is related to the session.

1. Write in the problem oval on the map the client's own problem after asking question (1): "What is the problem?"

     NOTE: *Ask for the specific problem related to the client's behavior: i.e. substance abuse.*

2. Write on the map the client's feelings, pressures, others' actions, and what led to the problem after asking question (2): What led to the problem?

3.   Then ask:

     What were your feelings about the problem? (starting question for women)

     What did others think about the problem?

     What did others do about the problem?

     What did you do about the problem? (starting question for men)

     NOTE: *Experience with this thought map by a number of persons indicates that the intervention will be most efficient if:*

     Men are first asked — What did you do about the problem? Their actions—which is followed by what others thought and what others did about their problem and ending with the question—What were your feelings about the problem?

     Women are first asked — What were your feelings about the problem?—which is followed by what others thought and what others did about their problem and ending with the question—What did you do about the problem?—Her actions.

4. Write in the appropriate box on the map the consequences of the problem after asking question (3): "What are the consequences of the problem," OR "What happened to you?"

5. Unfold the paper on the flip-chart so that the client can see the whole map. Tell the client that he is now going to look at a positive solution to this same problem—something he could have done differently that would have had positive consequences.

6. Write in the appropriate box on the map what the client says he could have done differently that would have made a positive change in the consequences after asking question (4): "What could you have done instead, to make the situation better?"

7. Write in the appropriate box on the map the consequences of the "better choice" after asking question (5): "What are the consequences of this positive choice?"

8. Write in the appropriate box on the map the client's feelings, pressures on him, others' actions, and his actions after asking question (6): "How will things be different as a result of your positive choice?"

9. Then ask:

What were your feelings about the solution? (starting question for women)

What would others think about the solution?

What would others do about the solution?

What would you do about the solution? (starting question for men)

NOTE: Remember to start with the feelings for women and actions for men when discussing how things would be different.

10. Write on the map the specific things the client says he can do to help solve the problem after asking question (7): What can you do now?

   - Remember to start with the problem, then the things that led to the problem, followed by the consequences and choice for solving the problem. Encourage the client to discuss a specific problem related to his own drug use. When the client talks about his problem behaviors, discuss the problem behavior by filling in the blanks on the map as the client talks.

   - Make sure enough time is allowed to reinforce the process. Point out that thought mapping is important before solving problems. Emphasize that most of the time there are several ways to deal with a problem. Make sure that the client hears the message that a small amount of time thinking about the consequences of their behavior can often avoid problems getting bigger.

   - Ask the client if he has any questions or comments? If he does, respond as directly as possible. If you do not know the answer to a question, say that you will find out the answer and get back to him with it.

A thought map guides and limits discussion. Blank maps help group discussion move rapidly toward causal links. Consequently, therapists need to be sensitive to pacing themselves with rural clients who tend to have some difficulty blaming family members or family situations. This does not mean that they should not be used with this population, only that skill and sensitivity should be used.

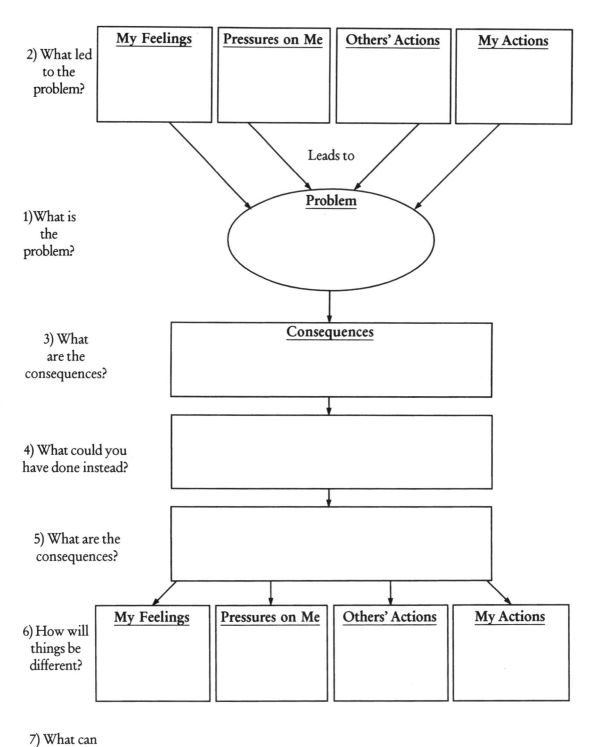

Figure 4.1: *Thought Map*

Example Thought Map

The following is an example of the use of a blank map in a group discussion with a client facing the problem of having lost visitation rights to his children.

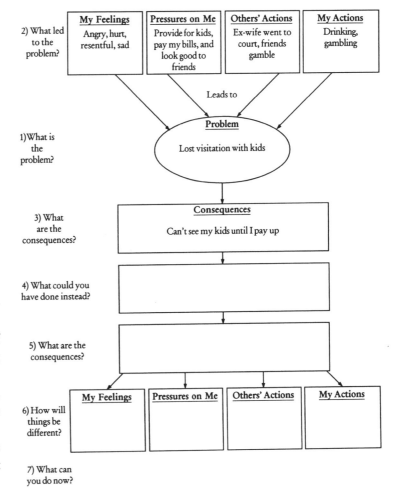

THERAPIST: Does anyone have a problem that they're willing to talk about in the group?

CLIENT 1: Yeah, I lost my visitation rights to my kids.

THERAPIST: That is a serious problem. What kinds of things led up to that?

CLIENT 1: I fell behind in my child support, my wife filed a complaint, we went to court and the judge said I didn't have the right to visit my kids until I paid up what I owe.

THERAPIST: How much are you behind in your child support?

CLIENT 1: $2,000.

THERAPIST: And how did you get so far behind?

CLIENT 1: I was doing a lot of gambling and drinking and lost a lot of money on the horses.

THERAPIST: Do you usually gamble a lot or is it something that you do when you're drinking?

CLIENT 1: The guys I drink with are heavy into gambling. It was just something everyone else was doing.

THERAPIST: Let me make sure I've got it right. You lost visitation rights to your kids because you fell pretty far behind in your child support. That happened because you lost money gambling and drinking. Your ex-wife's filing a complaint and what your drinking buddies do are part of the picture but not the cause of the problem.

CLIENT 1: Yeah, that's about right.

THERAPIST: Let me ask you what kinds of things in you, like feelings, pressures, and values, influenced your behavior.

CLIENT 1: Well, I wanted to fit in. You know how it is; my friends were all drinking and laying down bets and I didn't want to seem like, different or out of it. I guess I had some ideas about hitting a big score and getting ahead. But every time I did win, I just blew the winnings buying drinks for everybody. I guess I just wanted them to see me as some kind of big shot, or something.

THERAPIST: It seems that your drinking and gambling are problems you will have to face in some way if you're going to avoid problems like this in the future. (to Group:) What kinds of things can he do to deal with the present problem?

CLIENT 2: He can say to hell with everyone and leave town.

THERAPIST: OK, (to Client 1) is that something you would consider doing?

CLIENT 1: If I did that I wouldn't be any better than my father, I'd never have any kind of relationship with my kids.

THERAPIST: OK, if not leaving town, then what else?

CLIENT 4: He could borrow money and pay his back child support to get the court off his back.

THERAPIST: How's that?

CLIENT 1: Yeah, I could do that.

CLIENT 3: He could set aside money, like in a payroll savings plan, to pay off the back child support and make sure he stays even.

THERAPIST: (to Client 1) How's that?

CLIENT 1: Sounds all right.

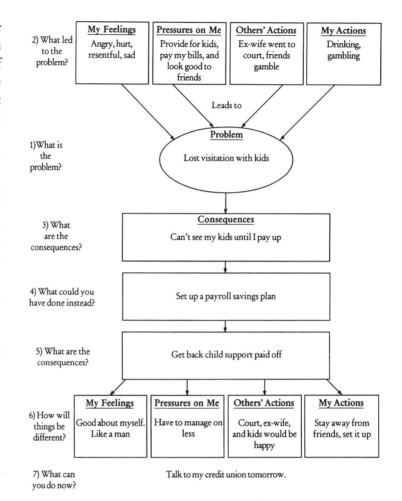

THERAPIST: What about borrowing the money?

CLIENT 5: It would be a quick fix, but he'd owe the money plus the interest. He might end up worse off.

THERAPIST: What about some sort of savings plan?

CLIENT 3: It would mean some sacrifice at first, not having the income. But once he adjusted it would be fairly painless and he could continue to use it to make sure he didn't fall behind again.

THERAPIST: Suppose you decide to borrow the money to pay off the back child support. How do you think doing that would affect your feelings?

CLIENT 1: I'd probably worry a lot about paying it back and keeping up with my regular child support.

THERAPIST: What about your values and pressures?

CLIENT 1: I'd still be dependent on somebody for the money.

THERAPIST: How do you think others would react to that decision?

CLIENT 1: I guess the judge would be happy, but if my ex-wife found out, she would worry about me just digging a deeper hole.

THERAPIST: What about setting up some kind of payroll savings plan?. How would that decision affect all those things?

CLIENT 1: Well, I guess I'd feel better about it and myself, like I was taking care of my own and standing on my own two feet. My ex-wife and kids would probably feel better about it since they would know

I was really trying to act responsible.

THERAPIST: What looks best to you?

CLIENT 1: A payroll savings plan makes the most sense.

THERAPIST: Is there anything that you are willing to do about that?

CLIENT 1: I could talk to the people down at my credit union about setting something up tomorrow.

The thought maps used in this manual for social skills training sessions follow the same structure. The central oval is where mapping begins. This central oval should contain a specific problem or an event. The boxes above the central node are for the circumstances and experiences that led up to, or preceded what is identified as the problem—specifically, the client's feelings, perceived pressures, actions, and the actions of others. The box below the central oval is for the consequences of the problem. These comprise the top half of the map and display what actually occurred.

The bottom half of the map examines what could be done differently (and more productively) in the future. The first box contains at least one alternative behavior that might be superior to a past behavior. The box below is for consequences that would likely occur as a result of the new, alternative action. The four smaller boxes directly below mirror the very top of the map by asking about the client's feelings, pressures, actions, and the actions of others—however, this time these are in response to the alternative behavior. Finally, at the bottom of the map, the client briefly states a feasible, "improved" plan of action.

The purpose of thought mapping is not only to help the client think about a specific problem, but to learn the process of effective problem solving. Some clients will need to work through several maps in order to figure out what might be a productive course of action. By patiently allowing the client to proceed in such a manner, the therapist is helping the client to learn an important new skill through repetition and practice.

Focus on possible responses to a problem, angry situation, or negative thought. The first box represents possible responses to the problem. Below is another box for the consequences of that response. It is important to identify and distinguish between short- and long-term consequences since they may be somewhat different. This is the case in the example above. The short-term consequence is fairly positive: getting right with the court and the children and getting visitation rights restored. The longer-term consequences are not as positive: still owing the original money plus interest.

Structured Storytelling

Storytelling has been called one of the building blocks of culture, like manufactured tools and cave painting (Schank, 1990). Storytelling was not simply an entertaining pastime. It enhanced both individual and group survival by improving memory and recall, allowing an efficient means of communicating, and retaining large amounts of information from generation to generation. Storytelling also helped our ancestors select effective actions to project from the past into the future (Rush, 1996). Just as language is related to the structure of the human mind (Chomski, 1957, 1968), storytelling is related to the structure of language. Language is a symbolic representation of experience, and storytelling is a representation of the relationships within that experience. Storytelling is a surprisingly sophisticated information-processing tool.

Storytelling is so much a part of our lives that we seldom think of it as something separate. If you ask a friend or acquaintance that you have not seen for some time how things have been, he will tell you at least one, if not several stories. If you go into a bookstore, you find shelves filled with stories. Even books that are labeled as technical or "how-to" contain some stories. If you decide you want passive entertainment, you will probably see stories on a television or movie screen. If you are a member of a self-help fellowship, such as AA, you go to meetings to share stories about what happened and what things are like now. If you are an attentive parent, storytelling is one of the earliest activities you share with your children. Stories are part of our lives.

There seems to be something special about stories and storytelling that commands attention and stimulates understanding. The most memorable part of a political speech is often a story told to gain the support and agreement of the audience. Even the most disruptive student in a classroom will usually settle down when the teacher reads or tells a story. The stories of mythic or national heroes are recounted time and again, often annually. Perhaps this is because stories and storytelling can involve us more than abstractions. Stories engage both cognition and affect in a uniquely powerful fashion that can make abstract realities accessible. Perhaps this is why spiritual teachers have used stories to communicate religious and moral information.

When telling a story, narrative experiences and relationships of those events and the relationship of each other are presented, and we express our understanding of the meaning and significance of those experiences. Thus, storytelling is an interpretive activity. When we tell personal stories, we are self-exploring, which can lead to insight into our behavior. It is these common experiences that stimulate similar thoughts in others. By hearing other stories, we can increase insight into behavior as well as recognize that behavior is not unique or isolated. For some reason, sharing common experiences creates a more positive perspective. This is the process that the founders of self-help groups instinctually discovered as helpful in changing behaviors. Further, if we change the way we tell a story, by modifying how we respond to specific experiences, we may create new behavioral possibilities in responding to those same experiences in our life. This is a kind of behavioral rehearsal that allows us to "try a new behavior."

Many of the social skills sessions in this manual involve storytelling to explore old behaviors and to try out new ones. Storytelling is included because our earlier work with rural therapists indicated that role-playing, the usual method of behavioral rehearsal in social skills training, was not as useful to rural clients. The method used here is not simply "swapping of yarns." Each story is structured to communicate the value of a specific social skill. Stories sometime illustrate negative consequences. However, most of the stories are not completed—they leave the protagonist in a situation where things can go either way depending on the decision made. This approach allows clients to explore connections between specific behavioral choices and specific outcomes.

When using structured storytelling, the therapist should insure that each story is presented in a way that illustrates the kinds of situations a specific social skill is meant to address. Therapists should also guide clients in understanding the relationship between a specific behavioral choice, the feelings or thoughts, as well as the consequences. Therapists also assist clients in recognizing that there are other behavioral choices which may be more or less desirable. Recognizing these choices can help clients use the story as a framework for exploring and practicing behavioral choices.

Using storytelling includes a brief introduction after which clients are asked if they have any personal stories related to the topic. In some groups, clients respond with relevant stories while in other groups, individuals are not able to tell their story. For situations when clients may be reluctant to volunteer stories or for those situations when the therapist feels it best to model storytelling, relevant stories are included. This process is called *priming the pump* because clients usually join in. The object is to engage rather than coerce clients to share stories. It is not necessary for every client to tell a story but to share experiences. The role of the therapist is to guide the process.

This process of "priming the pump" also involves modeling. The therapist presents not only the story narrative, but also the structure. This structure helps clients frame their own stories. "Prime the pump" stories present a specific problematic event in context (antecedents), relate the actions of the main character to this problem (behavior), and then relate or suggest a likely outcome (consequences). Stories also are designed to lead to better outcomes or avoid worse outcomes.

Therapists should not read "prime the pump" stories. Instead, therapists should familiarize themselves with these stories so that they can be told in an engaging way. The role of the therapist is to model storytelling, which precludes using a written text. Stories should be told in a straightforward manner in order to be engaging.

In some social skills training sessions, the therapist is asked to use stories to assist clients in gaining insights into their behaviors. This process may involve comparisons of stories on a common topic or it may involve a thought map. In other sessions, the therapist asks clients to modify their stories by inserting a different behavior and projecting a probable outcome. In both cases, the therapist assists clients to explore how their past behavior might be different and more successful in the future. Structured storytelling becomes a method for clients to explore a range of possible choices and a safe place for behavioral rehearsal of new behaviors.

Social Skills Sessions

After engaging, assessment, and behavioral contracting, clients are ready to begin the second phase of treatment: social skills training. Social skills training is an approach to drug and alcohol treatment that is based on cognitive-behavioral theory. Understanding the approach can help the therapist deliver effective social skills training groups.

The ideas behind cognitive-behavioral treatment are very different from expressive treatments like psychodynamic therapy. Instead of working with internal psychological structures like the "ego," behavioral theory focuses on how people learn specific behaviors over time. For example, children learn how to respond to social situations through watching their caregivers and then imitating what they see. This is not a planned process, but something that occurs quite naturally as the child grows. As the child experiments with such behaviors, a second powerful process occurs: the child's behavior is reinforced (causing an increase of that behavior's frequency) or the behavior is extinguished (causing a decrease and disappearance of the behavior). Such reinforcements can occur on many levels: the biological (e.g., experiences of physical pleasure), the interpersonal (e.g., receiving a compliment from another), the organizational (e.g., being awarded bonus pay), and the societal (e.g., receiving a tax break). This combination of watching, learning, imitating, and receiving a response from the environment is quite powerful and leads to new personal habits and automatic responses to situations.

Cognitive-behavioral theory stresses the integration of new skills within personal cognitive frameworks. Drug and alcohol users can have difficulty because of neurological damage sustained through use. Although often temporary, such deficits might last for several years—even if the person does not continue to use. Certainly, many clients will have only recently stopped or reduced drug and alcohol use, so their neurocognitive deficits might be significant. To account for this challenge, this therapy applies cognitive approaches (presenting information, using handouts) to the more complex approaches (i.e., thought mapping).

Why are the ideas behind behavioral and cognitive theory important to therapists working with drug- and alcohol-dependent clients? Monti (1989) explains the rationale for using social skills training to treat drug and alcohol problems:

> The central tenet of the coping skills approach to treatment is that through a variety of learning techniques (behavioral rehearsal, modeling, cognitive restructuring, didactic instruction), individuals and their social networks can be taught to use alternative methods of coping with demands of living without using maladaptive addictive substances such as alcohol.

Most important, this approach has been shown to be effective with urban clients struggling with drug and alcohol dependence. Structured Behavioral Outpatient Rural Treatment (SBORT) takes social skills training and modifies it for use with rural clients.

Every SBORT social skills group session has the same basic structure:

1. Group members should be introduced to any new member joining this session. The group begins with a quick review of the last session and, when appropriate, discussion of the last session's review exercise.

2. The therapist should discuss the "Message" of today's session and can list key points on a flip-chart or—ideally—use handouts.

3. The therapist should list and briefly discuss the "Skills" to be introduced and practiced in this group.

4. Next comes the "Group Exercise." Different sessions will include different exercises. For example, Session 4 includes a relaxation exercise, while Session 5 includes thought mapping and mutual storytelling.

5. Every group should end with distribution and discussion of a practice exercise.

Group Process

The group approach can be an effective way to treat clients for a number of clinical and economical reasons:

> The group approach is frequently more effective than the individual approach. This effectiveness stems from the fact that group members can practice new skills both within the group and in their everyday interactions outside of it. Moreover, members of the group benefit from feedback and insights of other group members as well as those of the practitioner. Groups also offer many opportunities for modeling. Members learn how to cope with their problems by observing others with similar concerns. There are practical reasons for the popularity of groups, too, such as lower costs and a broader distribution of the available therapists and therapists (Corey, 1995: 4).

SBORT incorporates the group process to teach social skills for all of the reasons above. Moreover, it is important to realize that these groups demand a very active leadership role on the part of the therapist. They are *structured*, i.e., they have a planned format with specific content. While different therapists will have different personal styles, the goal of the SBORT approach is to achieve a very high level of consistency for *what* content is delivered and *how* that content is delivered. *As you prepare for group, please be sure to follow this manual.* This can be difficult for therapists used to delivering their own educational or treatment materials. Some therapists might be tempted to discard sections of SBORT in favor of their own approach. It is important for the integrity of SBORT that each and every component is delivered in a way that reasonably adheres to the manual's instructions.

There are other reasons to prepare. For example, telling the "demonstration story" takes preparation—simply reading it is contraindicated because the therapist is trying to convey the content of the story, but also modeling that storytelling can be productive, interesting, fun, and meaningful. This takes preparation and practice before the therapist convenes the session.

Since there is a lot of material to be covered in each session, it will be difficult to attend to group dynamics and process if the therapist is not thoroughly familiar with the material itself. No matter how gifted or experienced the group therapist, there is no substitution for careful preparation. Clients will quickly detect the therapist who is "winging it," and unfortunately, might express their anger or amusement at this by disrupting the group. The prepared, confident therapist can handle a client who expresses negative emotions or opinions by focusing on the client's reactions as he relates to the material or some other client-centered reason. In contrast, the highly anxious therapist might see clients such as these as a threat and be unable to therapeutically manage such interactions. Additionally, careful preparation—including the use of prepared overheads or flip-charts—can keep the group running on time and in an orderly fashion. This not only makes the content more understandable, but it creates an atmosphere of stability that can allow clients to focus on their work. Many clients will need the opportunity to ask questions and review materials. Good preparation will allow the therapist to repeat key points in a consistent manner. Finally, the well-prepared therapist can relax and allow the spontaneity of group work to emerge, i.e., the different personalities and temperaments of group members can be encouraged to make group sessions interesting, lively, and memorable.

The therapist must carefully assess the cognitive abilities of the group—especially noting which group members might have more difficulty with written materials or graphics. Certain groups might require a slower pace than others. Although the group process relies on verbal skills, reading and writing activities are also incorporated in the sessions. Extra assistance for members struggling with this approach should be given so that those group members are not humiliated or excluded because of their cognitive limitations.

Practice Exercises

Cognitive difficulties might compromise a client's participation and compliance with practice exercises. While the experience of learning new skills during the social skills group sessions is critical, the experience of practicing these skills outside the group is equally important. A central principle of cognitive-behavioral therapy is that skill acquisition is retained primarily by behavioral repetition. Practice exercises provide a structured way to do this. Monti points out that practice is a powerful adjunct to group sessions since it "offers the distinct advantage of practice in actual problem situations" (1989: 136). Practice also makes the client "generalize" the skill to settings outside of group, in their everyday settings where they can use the skills to maintain recovery.

Group practice exercises focus on one or two skills introduced during the group session. Clients are given a reminder sheet, which "cues" the specific behavior for the client to practice. Clients are also given the practice sheet, which "walks them through" the practice and can be used to note what happened when they tried the exercise.

There are several approaches the therapist can use to encourage clients to complete exercises:

1. Use the term "practice"; avoid the negative term "homework." Practice allows a number of non-academic analogies (e.g., sports, music, crafts).

2. Take time during the group session to explain the practice exercise. Give the reason for the exercise and answer questions.

3. Ask group members to generate reasons why they might not complete the exercise. Join them

in a discussion of how such obstacles can be overcome. Generate pragmatic strategies.

4. Review practice exercises from the previous session at the beginning of each group session. Avoid the teacher-student dynamic. We suggest that therapists use a "co-investigator" approach of exploring with clients the results of their "experiment" in real-life settings.

5. Praise completed assignments. Praise all approximations to completion and encourage completion. Discuss reasons for not completing with persons who did not try the exercise, but do not humiliate them. Monti (1989) recommends that therapists avoid the use of material rewards for success; the key is to let persons who do not work on the practice exercises learn that completers receive praise.

Helping Cognitively Challenged Clients

Drug and alcohol therapists recognize that many of their clients have experienced temporary or permanent damage from their substance abuse that can compromise cognitive performance. Other clients never learned the cognitive skills they need to succeed as adults, as noted in the following examples:

1. Susan is addicted to marijuana and alcohol. While she can read and write, she finds it difficult to retain information for very long. She finds herself quickly bored by such tasks.

2. Mike used inhalants and amphetamines for many years. He now complains that it is almost impossible for him to read and follow written instructions.

3. Teddy is dyslexic, but this was never recognized when he was in school. He has never learned to read or write beyond the Grade Two level.

It is important for the therapist to detect clients who are struggling with the cognitive tasks included in the SBORT treatment. For example, some clients might habitually not complete practice exercises because of such problems. Others might "act up" in group sessions because they cannot process written or mapped information. Therapists should differentiate between those who resist the treatment process because they are not ready and those who are ready but cognitively challenged.

What can therapists do to help manage clients with cognitive deficits? Here are some approaches to use:

1. When you identify a client with such problems, arrange to meet with her individually. At the meeting gently explore the issue by citing a few examples of what you have seen her do or fail to do. You might open the issue of cognitive problems by saying, "Many people who have drug and alcohol problems tell me that they have trouble reading or understanding the material I am teaching. I was wondering if you are having such difficulties."

2. Be patient. The client may feel anxious and/or angry with this issue. Use the motivational-interview approach of active listening. The client may need some time to deal with your concerns. Many adults feel humiliated by their cognitive deficits.

Above all, don't get frustrated. Maintain a positive "problem-solving" attitude.

Skills Session 1: Managing Thoughts and Fantasies about Alcohol and Drugs

Information for Therapists:

The purpose of this session is to discuss and identify thoughts and fantasies about drug and alcohol use, as well as the feelings that they can evoke. This session helps participants explore how thoughts and fantasies might lead to relapse so that each client can develop beliefs and skills to manage thoughts and fantasies productively.

It is helpful for clients to understand that long-term use of any drug causes changes in the structure and function of the brain. These changes are the underlying cause of both thoughts and fantasies about drug use as well as urges and cravings. Although the subject matter is a bit complicated, it is worth the effort to assist clients in understanding these changes and the effect they have on individuals who have used drugs over a long period of time and then stopped use. In order to do this effectively, it is important to have an understanding of these matters.

Message to Clients:

Having thoughts, fantasies, and dreams about using alcohol and drugs can be very troubling for people in early stages of recovery. These thoughts and fantasies are rooted in changes that take place in the brain as a result of the long-term drug use, as well as the associations that are formed between pleasurable alteration in brain chemistry and various situations, persons, and experiences.

Fortunately, having thoughts, fantasies, and dreams does not indicate that a person will relapse. In fact, these mental experiences are a *normal* part of the recovery process. At the same time, it is critical that recovering persons learn to understand and deal with their thoughts and fantasies in a way that helps them resist acting upon them and relapsing.

Thoughts and fantasies may be related to specific situations, such as:

- Local drug-use customs,

- A desire to test control,

- Life crisis situations,

- Feelings of discomfort when abstinent, and

- Feelings of doubt about the ability to recovery.

Skills:

People can develop the following particular beliefs and skills, which can help them manage such mental experiences:

- Thoughts of using drugs and alcohol again are "normal" in recovery.

- Having thoughts about using does not mean a relapse.

- Acting on or giving in to thoughts about using is the problem, not having those thoughts.

- There are common thoughts that have been found to be manageable.

- Knowing which thoughts and fantasies are likely for each person can help to keep them from using.

The isolation of rural communities with few transportation options makes it difficult for persons to leave situations or change activities. A rural person may also have limited ways of communicating and may have limited use of a telephone to call another person to support their recovery. The therapist can help address such environmental challenges by asking group members how others have overcome these obstacles, and by sharing experiences using stories about how other rural people have solved these problems, such as using an AA/NA sponsor and developing diverting activities available to rural people.

Group Exercise:

1. Begin the session by talking to the clients about the effects that long-term drug use can have on the brain. Make the link between changes that occur in brain structure and function and the experiences of thoughts and fantasies about drug use, as well as urges and cravings to return to drug use.

   NOTE TO THERAPISTS: *Use transparencies as a visual aid for clients. Begin with a presentation similar to the following:*

   "You may never have thought about it, but we carry around the most complex system of communication and information processing ever known: our brain. Everything that we experience—whether a physical sensation like the smell of the woods on a spring morning, the sight of a field of wildflowers blooming, or an internal experience like love, fear, or sense of anticipation—takes place right there. Inside each of our heads is a network of electrochemical interaction so complex that, even with all that we have learned in the past, we barely begin to understand. I want to talk to you today about that network we call the brain and about the effect that the use of drugs has on it. If you should find yourself confused, or having difficulty understanding, please let me know so we can discuss it.

   "Our bodies are made up of a very large number of cells. Cells are the basic building blocks of all living things. The most important cells in our brains are called neurons. Neurons have a very special ability, they can communicate with one another in a kind of electrochemical language.

"There are a very large number of neurons in our brains—about 100 million. It's an unimaginably large number—about the same as the estimated number of stars in the Milky Way galaxy. Each of these neurons is able to communicate with up to 10,000 other neurons. Think about neurons as telephone lines. Imagine that each of those 100 billion people has a direct telephone line to between 10 and 10,000 other people so that any time they want they can pick up that line and talk to some or all of the people they are connected to at the same time. Not only that, but they all speak the same language, and they can talk as loudly or as softly as they want and always be understood.

"Neurons look something like this."

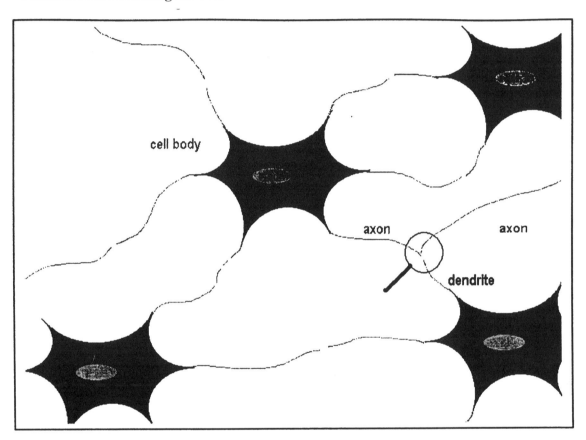

"The main part of a neuron is called the 'cell body.' This part of the neuron carries on the same business as any other living cell: it digests food, excretes waste products, absorbs oxygen, and divides (at least in the early part of its life) to make new neurons. Extending out from the cell body there are arms that look a little like tentacles. It is along these 'arms' that messages travel from one neuron to another. The arms that <u>send</u> messages are called 'axons,' and the arms that <u>receive</u> messages are called 'dendrites.' The neurons are able to do something that most cells can't do—generate their own electrical charge. The messages from one neuron to another are in the form of an electrical current. The neurons can change the frequency (the number of electrical messages they send per second) and the amplitude (the strength or volume of their electrical signal or both)."

(Use the above illustration to give concrete meaning to the explanation that follows:)

"When one neuron sends a message to another neuron the electrical signal flows along the axon of that neuron until it reaches the end of the axon. Near the end of the axon of one neuron is the receiving arm or dendrite of another neuron. Now, these two do not touch, they are not like electrical wires in your house that are twisted or soldered together. There is a space between the axon of one neuron and the dendrite. This space is called a 'synapse.' The electrical message from one neuron to another has to cross this space, and that's where chemicals come in.

"The space where one neuron makes contact with another is represented in the following drawing:"

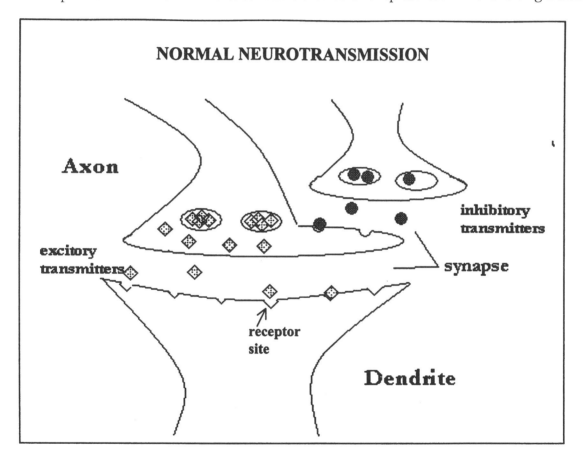

"At the sending end, or axon, of a neuron there are chemicals called 'neurotransmitters.' They're called that because they transmit the information across that space or synapse from one neuron to another.

"The electrical signals cause some of these transmitter chemicals to be released into the space between the neurons. They cross that space and fit into 'receptor sites' on the receiving end or dendrite of the next neuron just like a key fits into a lock. When they do that, they set off a reaction in the next neuron, which causes it to receive, change, or continue the flow of that electrical message. Now, there are two kinds of transmitter chemicals: 'excitatory transmitters,' represented by the diamond-shaped figures in the drawing and 'inhibitory transmitters,' represented by the round-shaped figures in the drawing. The excitatory transmitters are called that because they excite the next neuron, they crank it up to continue the signal or even turn up the volume of the signal. The inhibitory transmitters are called that because they inhibit, or turn down, the volume on the signal. Understanding how these two types of transmitters work is important because both of them come into play when we try to understand how drug use affects brain function.

"All of us have a lot of experience with these two types of transmitters even though we don't think about it in these terms. For example, have you ever had the experience of hammering in a nail, missing the nail, and hitting your thumb with the hammer? Remember how when you first hit your thumb, it really hurts. You drop the nail, shake your hand, and swear a lot. Well, stop and think; after a few seconds the pain tends to get less, doesn't it? And a few seconds after that the pain is almost gone and your thumb may even feel a little numb. In no time at all you're looking for the nail you dropped and have gone back to pounding, probably with a little more caution. What I've just described is an experience in neurotransmission. When you first hit your thumb with the hammer, a pain message goes to your brain at about the speed of light. The message is very strong. Neurons in your brain get the message, process the information, and send back a set of signals to your hand. These signals inform your muscles to stop hammering, get rid of the nail, and shake your hand to increase blood flow to your injured thumb. At the same time, other messages go out, rerouting blood flow, causing you to hop up and down, and activating your speech apparatus to swear. All of these signals involve excitatory transmitters that move the messages and get action fast. Pain messages keep coming in from your thumb to your brain and pretty soon the brain neurons begin to turn down the volume on these signals. It's like the brain is saying, 'OK, I get the message! I've done everything I can for right now!' Within another second or two, more subtle messages get to the brain informing the neurons there about the extent of the damage. Since the damage isn't bad, the neurons turn down the pain signals even further so that you can get back to work. This entire turning down of signals is the work of inhibitory transmitters. Now it really is amazing how quickly and efficiently all this information flows back and forth and how quickly it is processed. Do all of you follow me so far?"

(Respond to any questions or confusion so that you make sure there is a basic understanding of how neurotransmission works.)

"What does this have to do with drugs? Well, it has everything to do with drugs. Did you ever think about where drugs come from? What about opium, morphine, and heroin? Where do they all come from?"

(See if anyone knows.)

"They come from the sap of poppy flowers. What about alcohol? Where does alcohol come from? How do you make it?"

(See if anyone knows.)

"To make alcohol you take any liquid that contains a lot of sugar. It doesn't matter where it comes from. It can be from grape or berry juice. It can be from half-sprouted grain. It can even come from sugar cane. You take that liquid and you put "little creatures" in it called yeast. Yeast is not exactly plant or animal but it does one thing very well: eat sugar and excrete alcohol. Those yeast cells go to work on that sugar gorging themselves on it, multiplying, and excreting alcohol. They do that until there are so many of them eating that sugar and excreting alcohol that they eventually die in their own waste. You can drink that liquid just the way it is and have just plain old yeast waste product (you can call it wine or beer), or you can distill it down and have concentrated yeast waste product (you can call that bourbon or gin or vodka). In either case, alcohol is simply a waste product from the yeast.

"Now you have to ask yourself, why should the sap of some flower or the waste product of some tiny creature like yeast have the effect it has when we put it into our bodies? The simple truth is that these chemicals are like chemicals or affect the action of chemicals that already exist in our bodies, primarily in our brains, and specifically our transmitters. All the drugs that people get messed up on either can substitute for our own natural neurotransmitters or can affect how our neurotransmitters act. Remember when I said that the transmitters, when they cross that space between the sending end of one neuron and the receiving end of another neuron, fire into receptor sites like a key fits into a lock. Well, drugs, at least many of them, are like skeleton keys that can fit into those same locks, those same receptor sites. When they do that, they affect the whole process of communication in the brain, and we call that 'drug effect.'

"To help understand that, look at this next slide."

DRUG AFFECTED NEUROTRANSMISSION

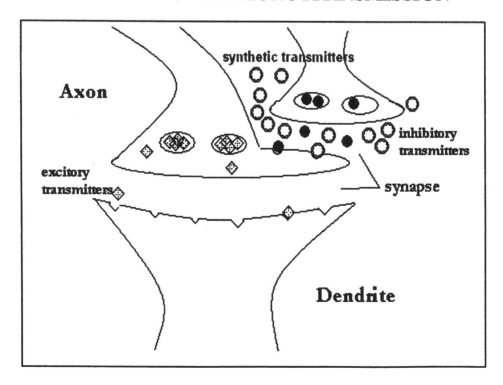

"Notice that we have added a lot of round shapes to this drawing, which are called 'synthetic transmitters.' These represent a drug like Valium or one of the opiate drugs that act as if they were inhibitory transmitters. They flood the spaces between neurons and occupy all the receptor sites that would be used by inhibitory transmitters. Notice what has happened in this picture to the excitatory transmitters, those that are represented by diamond shapes. There are fewer of them being released to carry the message from one neuron to another. This is just what happens with these types of drugs: they turn down the volume on the transmission of messages from one neuron to another. Your ability to react to things is changed since the effect of the drug is to slow down your reflexes; consequently, you're a danger if you get behind the wheel of a car or operate farm machinery. Some people really like this sort of experience because the drug creates the illusion that 'life is wonderful' and all needs have been met. This is why drugs like the opiates and Valium are sometimes called 'satiation' type drugs. If you continue to take more of these drugs, the rate of the transmission will slow down enough so that you will become unconscious. Beyond that point, the slowdown of transmission between neurons may become so serious that you stop breathing or your heart stops beating. This is what happens in an overdose with these kinds of drugs. Like all living things, neurons have the ability to change and to adapt to whatever is going on around them. That's exactly what happens to the neurons in the brain of someone who regularly uses drugs. The neurons adapt to the presence of the drug. The next slide presents one way that neurons adapt and change."

DRUG ADAPTED NEUROTRANSMISSION

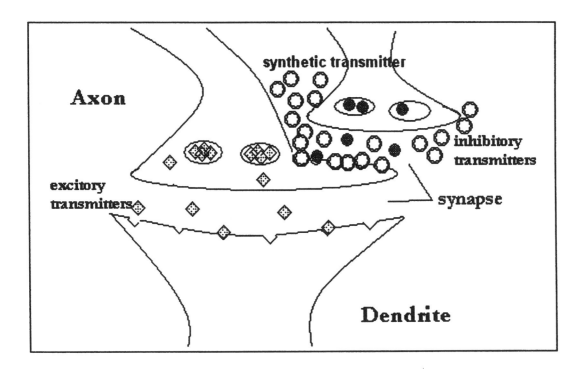

"Notice how, in this slide, the axon, the sending end of the neuron, has developed more receptor sites for the synthetic transmitter, the drug. When the drug is present on a regular basis over time, the neuron responds by growing more receptor sites for the drug to fit into. As this happens, more of the drug is usually needed in the system to get that satiation effect. This is called *tolerance*. All of you have experienced that as you use a drug over time; you tend to need more of that drug to get the same effect. As a matter of fact, a person may start to feel uncomfortable, jumpy, tense, and anxious rather than calm and peaceful like when you were first using.

"It is important that you understand that all of this is not just 'psychological.' It involves *real changes* in the structure of the cells that make up the brain. As changes take place in some of the neurons of the brain, it affects how communications take place all through the brain. Everything starts to change. Over time, your ability to think, to plan, to value, to feel, to experience, to act, to you name it begins to change. None of us is separate from our brain. What kind of person you are, what is important to you, how you see the world, what you consider right or wrong is all bound up in how your brain works. If you change how your brain functions in any significant way, you quite literally change who you are. One of the most obvious changes is that getting and using the drug becomes more and more important to you. It may become more important than eating, or sleeping, or earning a living, or taking care of your children. You stop doing things that you used to enjoy. Things that used to be important to you hardly get a second thought. Things that you used to take pride in, no longer matter to you. You now do what you used to disapprove of. People you might have avoided in the past, now become your closest friends. You are no longer the person you were before you started using drugs. You have become someone different because the use of the drugs changed the way in which your brain functions and is structured. These changes are the process of addiction.

"Let's say that one day, for whatever reason, you decide to stop using drugs. This next slide gives you a picture of what the neurons are like.

NEUROTRANSMISSION IN EARLY RECOVERY

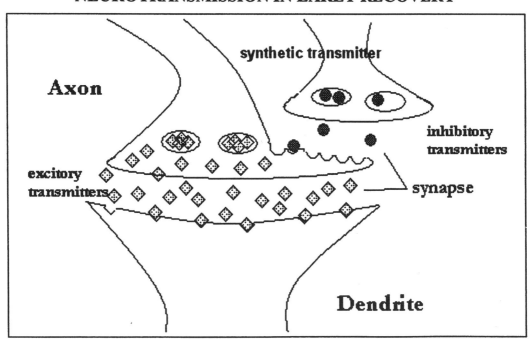

"Notice that all the synthetic transmissions—the drug—are gone. However, the extra receptor sites that the neuron grew to adjust to the presence of the drug are still there. Notice, too, what happens to the excitatory transmitter. It has not just gone to normal levels but is well above normal. The volume has been turned up to well above the level it was at before the drug use. If this happens to an extreme degree, it can lead to serious symptoms that are called *withdrawal.* In a general sort of way, the withdrawal symptoms from any drug are the exact opposite of the effect of the drug. We have been talking about Valium so let's stick with that. If you have been taking Valium at high doses for a long time and then you stop taking it, you may experience any or all of these symptoms: anxiety, difficulty sleeping, agitation, agitated depression, and seizure. Withdrawal symptoms happen within a few hours to a few days after someone stops using drugs and they last for a few days to a few weeks. Most people don't experience any life-threatening withdrawal symptoms when they stop using, but they sure can feel uncomfortable. Even after initial withdrawal is over, the changes that have taken place in the structure and function of the neurons and of the brain itself do not disappear.

"Understanding the experience of someone who has used drugs for a while, has experienced changes in the functioning of the neurons and the brain as a result of that drug use, and has stopped using drugs is not difficult if you just think about it a little. If you find yourself in that situation, consider the fact that you started using the drug because you found the effect pleasurable and positive. You liked feeling the way the drug made you feel. You used the drug often enough to bring about some pretty major changes in your brain that caused having the drug and using the drug to become central to your life. Over time, your life rearranged around your drug use so that almost everywhere you turn you are reminded of using the drug. Most of what you have done in the recent past involved using; most of the people you have been with in the recent past use; and things and people that don't have to do with drug use don't much interest you just yet. Is it any wonder that you think about using a lot, that you remember every positive experience you ever had with a drug as if it were yesterday, that you fantasize about using, and that you even dream about using?

"Another way to think about all of this is to compare the drug to food or water. Your brain is geared to give very high priority to having adequate food and water. Of course, this is because you need food and water to survive. When you feel hungry or thirsty, you start thinking about getting something to eat or drink. Having food or water becomes a priority. Suppose you decide that you need to lose weight—you need to cut back on the amount of food you eat and the kinds of food you eat. When you begin, you find that you feel hungry often and that even when you do eat you're not satisfied. After a few days on this diet, what do you suppose you might be thinking about a lot of the time? What kinds of fantasies do you think you might be having? What kinds of things will you dream about? You've got it—FOOD. Not only food in general but also exactly the kind of food you don't need if you want to lose weight. Well, if you have used drugs enough to change the function of your brain, then the drugs have taken on the same status for you as food and water. When the drugs aren't there, you react as if you were dying of hunger or thirst. Of course, the drugs are not at all necessary for your survival in the way food and water are. As a matter of fact, the drugs may be very bad for your survival. That doesn't stop your altered brain from reacting in the same way it would to being starved or dying of thirst.

"The important thing to understand is that having thoughts and fantasies about drugs is normal in early recovery because of the abnormal state of your brain and neurons. The condition is temporary. Just as the neurons adjusted to the presence of the drug and that set in motion a domino effect that changed the brain, consequently the neurons will adapt to the absence of the drug, returning to a more normal state. This change will have an effect on the whole brain as well. However, these changes take time. You really can't do much about the physical changes that will happen in your neurons and your brain except to take reasonably good care of yourself. Just commonsense measures like eating right, getting enough sleep, and having an appropriate level of exercise will really help. And while these changes are taking place, there are also things that you can do to help you deal with the thoughts and fantasies about drug use, as well as the urges and craving. We will be spending the next two sessions talking about doing just that. However, there's no magical solution to any of this, but there are things you can do that are genuinely helpful."

2. After the presentation, ask clients if they have any questions or comments. Invite discussing their own experiences to see if they confirm what you have said. Take the time to insure that clients understand what you have told them and assist them in achieving the best understanding possible. Once you feel that you have done this, move to the next part of this session, which uses storytelling as a way to communicate skills necessary for dealing with thoughts and fantasies about drug use.

3. The therapist "primes the pump" by telling a story about thoughts and fantasies. Group members are asked to compare stories of specific times and places they had thoughts of using when they were trying to not use in a rural community. They are also asked to discuss when and how these thoughts occurred.

Prime the Pump:

By introducing a story, the therapist models the importance of telling stories that focus on the targeted social skill. The therapist primes the pump, and group members begin to tell their own stories. For example, here is a story about fantasies and thoughts about drug and alcohol use:

"Jack used a lot of alcohol and Valium ever since he was in high school. He graduated from high school, got a job at the local factory, and married his high school sweetheart. He didn't have many problems at first because he never used on the job, but his wife, Denise, also liked using. In fact, they felt close as a couple because of the great parties they had on the weekends. Things went well until Denise discovered she was pregnant. She decided that she had to stop using because she was afraid that her baby would be deformed if she didn't. (One of her cousins had been damaged that way and had died at age 12. She was able to get Jack to agree to stop using, too. At first he stopped, but then he started using behind her back. She caught him and told him that she would leave him and move back home if he didn't clean up his act. This happened two more times, and they were barely talking.

"Then his work at the factory went downhill. (He had been drinking and drugging on the job since he couldn't use at home anymore.) His foreman said he had to get into treatment, or he would be fired. So Jack began to go to AA and to the local treatment center for counseling. He didn't like it at first but then began to do O.K., especially since he was better.

"Jack did pretty well with recovery. He liked the fact that he was going to be a father and began to use the extra money they had from not using to buy things for the baby. When the baby came, he was very excited—she was a healthy baby girl. But then things got tough. Denise was wrapped up with the baby and Jack began to feel left out. Denise had to have a C-section, so they couldn't have sex immediately. Besides, the baby slept in their bed at night. The baby was colicky, so Jack was getting only a few hours of sleep each night. On top of this, he was working overtime. Jack began to feel worn out, sick, and lonely. He felt that his nerves were shot.

"He began thinking about how great life had been in high school and in the first year he and Denise were married. He remembered the great parties they had enjoyed and how free and easy life had been. He ran into a friend he used to drink and drug with, and his friend asked if Jack wanted to go over to his place after work. Jack initially refused but then began to imagine how great it would be to just have a few drinks and relax—maybe even get some sleep. He couldn't get his mind off it his whole shift. When he got home, the baby was screaming. Denise laid into him about needing to help more around the house."

4. Ask group members for stories and talk about situations, in the past, when they had thoughts that led to using. Ask group members to compare experiences.

   NOTE TO THERAPISTS: *Common situations can include feelings of being stressed, bored, lonely, tired, angry, or depressed; feeling sexually aroused or deprived; or holidays, weekends, and other celebrations. Specific situations in rural areas can be unemployment, too much free time, thinking or talking about using, or being around people who are using or talking about using since "escape" from a situation can be harder in rural areas.*

5. Ask group members to talk about *when* these thoughts are most common.

6. Examine the pros and cons of using drugs. Ask group members to make a list of their own benefits of using and the problems or risks they have encountered from using. Use the following example or one similar:

Pros (+)	Cons (-)
1)	1)
2)	2)
3)	3)

7. Observe the negative list. Can it be divided by listing at least three *immediate* negative things that can happen, and three things that can be *delayed?*

8. Group members are then asked to write these lists on index cards provided for the group. Carrying the lists with them can be helpful. Ask group members to recall risks and benefits whenever they find themselves thinking or daydreaming about using.

9. List techniques currently used by clients on a flip-chart or blackboard. Make the following list of skills for managing thoughts and fantasies and discuss.

- Challenging the thought or fantasy.

- Recalling the benefits of not using drugs.

- Recalling unpleasant events while using.

- Distracting with an activity.

- Reinforcing current success.

- Delaying the decision at least 15 minutes.

- Leaving the situation or changing activities.

- Calling someone who is supportive of you.

10. Check in with the group to see if any client is currently having difficulty managing thoughts and fantasies. If a client is having difficulty, have the client use the previously discussed skills while in the group so that the client doesn't leave the session wanting to use drugs.

11. At the end of the session, distribute Handout 1 and discuss expectations for completing the practice exercise by the next time the group meets.

Adapted from Monti, Peter M. et al (1989). Treating Alcohol Dependence. *New York: Guilford Press (79–83).*

Skills Session 1—Handout 1: MANAGING THOUGHTS AND FANTASIES ABOUT DRUG USE

Reminder Sheet
The following are several ways of managing thoughts about drugs and alcohol:

1. Challenge your thoughts: Do you really need to use?

2. Will you really not have fun without using?

3. Think of the benefits of not using.

4. Remember unpleasant using experiences and aftereffects.

5. Distraction: Think of something unrelated to using.

6. Positive thinking: Remind yourself of your success.

7. Use images of riding out the craving until it passes.

8. Use images of loved ones who would be disappointed if you use.

9. Delaying the decision technique: Put off the decision to use for 15 minutes or more. Try using "images" until the urge to use passes.

10. Leave or change the situation.

11. Call someone and try to talk it out.

Practice Exercise:
One way of coping with thoughts about using is to remind yourself about the benefits of not using and the unpleasant effects of using.

Benefits *of using drugs* and alcohol:

_____
_____

Benefits *of not using* drugs and alcohol:

_____
_____

Unpleasant effects *of using* drugs and alcohol:

_____
_____

Unpleasant effects *of not using* drugs and alcohol:

_____
_____

Adapted from Monti, P.M. et al. (1989). Treating Alcohol Dependence. *New York: Guilford (211).*

Skills Session 2: Coping with Cravings and Urges

Information for Therapists:

In rural areas, coping with craving triggers can be difficult, because there is often no way to avoid them. Residents of rural areas generally place high regard on family, and if there is significant family drug or alcohol use, it may be difficult to escape triggers. It is unlikely that the newly recovering person will make a choice to avoid "kin" totally (Keefe, 1988; Looff, 1971). In small communities it can also be difficult to avoid contact with people, places, and situations associated with drug use, simply because of geography. There aren't as many people to choose from for friends, and there aren't as many places to go as there are in urban areas. Recovery resources can also be limited. Thus, relying on self-monitoring and encouraging personal independence and individualism can be important to establish a pattern of recognizing and coping with craving.

Message to Clients:

Craving is most often experienced early in recovery, but episodes of craving may persist for weeks or even years. Although craving is an uncomfortable experience, it is quite common and does not mean something is wrong. Craving can be anticipated and coping can be learned. Urges to use and cravings can be triggered by things in the environment that are reminders of using, physical and psychological experiences like feelings of anxiety or boredom, or memories of past positive experiences of drug use. Poor diet and nutrition can also contribute to increased craving. Keep in mind that cravings and urges are time-limited and become less frequent and intense as coping skills are learned.

Skills:

Emphasize the following three skills:

1. Recognize Triggers:

    - Exposure to alcohol or drugs

    - Seeing others use

    - Contacts with particular people, places, times of day, and situations, which can include drinking and drugging buddies, parties, holidays, bars, getting home from work, certain music, having large amounts of cash in your pocket, and weekends in general.

    - High-sugar foods (alcohol dependence is positively associated with strong sweet consumption)

    - Certain physical feelings like feeling sick, shaky, and pain.

- Specific emotions:

- Negative feelings, particularly anger, frustration, fatigue, and feeling stressed out, lonely, sad, guilty, anxious or bored.

- Positive emotions like elation, excitement, and feelings that make you want to celebrate.

- Using medicines prescribed to you by a doctor, even if you use them properly.

- Believing that you are finally cured; that getting high won't bother you anymore.

2. Monitoring triggers is important for dealing with them.

- The easiest way to deal with cravings and urges is to avoid them. Reducing exposure to triggers can help. This could include getting rid of paraphernalia, alcohol in the house, a stash of drugs, not going to bars and parties, and reducing contact with people who use.

3. Sometimes craving cannot be avoided, and it is necessary to find a way to cope with it. Some strategies for dealing with cravings include:

- *Getting involved in a distracting activity.* Reading, a hobby, going to a movie, and exercising are examples. Once a person gets interested in something else, urges go away.

- *Talking it through.* Talking to friends or family members about the cravings when they occur can be helpful in pinpointing the source of the craving. Talking about cravings can also help a person feel closer to others. It is important to choose someone who can accept and understand that craving is a normal part of the recovery process and not be frightened or angry about the presence of cravings. A sponsor (AA or NA) can be helpful.

- *Urge surfing.* Many people try to cope with their cravings by gritting their teeth and "toughing it out," especially when craving comes from exposure to triggers like old environments. These cravings can be very strong. When faced with strong urges, it can be helpful to just stay with the urge to use until it passes.

  Urges have been described as ocean waves. They are small when they start, grow in size, and then break up and go away. A person can imagine him/herself as a surfer who rides the wave, staying on top of it until it crests, breaks, and turns into less powerful, foamy surf. The idea behind urge surfing is similar to the idea behind many martial arts. In judo, a person overpowers an opponent by first going with the force of the attack. By joining with the opponent's force, a person can take control of it and redirect it to an advantage. This technique of gaining control by first going with the opponent also allows one to take control while expending minimal energy. Urge surfing is similar. A person can initially join with an urge, as opposed to meeting it as a strong force, as a way of taking control of it. After a person practices urge surfing several times and becomes familiar with it, it can be a useful technique to cope with urges.

There are four steps in urge surfing:

1. *Take an inventory of how the craving is experienced.* Do this by sitting in a comfortable chair with your feet flat on the floor and your hands in a comfortable position. Take a few deep breaths and focus your attention inward. Allow your attention to wander through your body. Notice where in your body you experience the craving and what the sensations are like. Notice each area where you experience the urge, and tell yourself what you are experiencing. For example, "Let me see . . . My craving is in my mouth, nose, and in my stomach."

2. *Focus on one area where cravings are experienced.* Notice the exact sensations in that area. For example, do you feel hot, cold, tingly, or numb? Are your muscles tense or relaxed? How large an area is involved? Notice the changes that occur in the sensation. "Well, my mouth feels dry and parched. There is tension in my lips and tongue. I keep swallowing. As I exhale, I can imagine the smell and tingle of the drugs."

3. *Repeat the focusing with each body part that experiences the craving.* Pay attention to, and describe to yourself, the changes that occur in the sensations. Notice how the urge comes and goes. Many people, when they urge surf, notice that after a few minutes the craving has vanished. However, the purpose of this exercise is not to make the craving go away but to experience the craving in a new way. If you practice urge surfing, you will become familiar with your cravings and learn how to ride them out until they go away.

4. *Challenge and change thoughts.* When experiencing a craving, many people have a tendency to remember only the positive effects of using drugs and often forget the negative consequences of drinking and drugging. Therefore, when experiencing craving, many people find it helpful to remind themselves of the benefits of not drinking and the negative consequences of drinking. It is helpful to have a list of these benefits and consequences on a small card that you can keep with you. This way, you can remind yourself that you really won't "feel better if you just use once" and that you stand to lose a lot by the relapse.

   People constantly appraise and think about things that happen to them and the things that they do. The way that you feel and act can be as highly influenced by these subjective facts or appraisals as well as objective facts. What you tell yourself about your urges to use will affect how you experience and handle them.

   Your "self-talk" can be put to use to strengthen or weaken your urges. The process of making self-statements becomes so automatic by the time you are an adult, you may not notice that you do this. It simply does not require any attention now. A self-statement that has become automatic for you is, "The big hand is on the 7, so it is 35 minutes after. The little hand is between the 2 and 3, so it is 2 o'clock. That means that the time is 2:35." Instead, you automatically read the clock to tell time. Hidden or automatic self-statements about urges and cravings can make them harder to handle. For example, "Now I want a drink. I won't be able to stand this. The urge is going to keep getting stronger and stronger until I blow up or use." Other types of self-statements can make the urge easier to handle. For example, "Even though my mind is made up to stay sober, my body will take a while to learn this. This urge is uncomfortable, but in 15 minutes or so, I'll be feeling like myself again."

There are two basic steps to use self-talk constructively:

1. *Pinpoint what you tell yourself about an urge that makes it harder to cope with the urge.* One way to tell if you are on the right track is finding a self-statement that increases your discomfort. That discomfort-raising self-statement is a leading suspect for challenge, since you react to it.

2. *Use self-talk constructively to challenge an internal statement.* An effective challenge will make you feel better—less tense, anxious, and panicky—even though it may not make the feelings disappear entirely. The most effective challenges are those that are tailored to your specific upsetting self-statements. Several challenges that have been found to be useful include:

    •   What is the evidence that if you didn't have a drink in the next 10 minutes, you will die? Has anyone ever died from not drinking?

    •   What's so terrible about experiencing an urge? If you hang in there, you will feel fine. These urges are not like being hungry or thirsty, they are more like a craving for candy. They will pass.

    •   You are a regular human being and have a right to make mistakes. Maybe you worry about being irritable, preoccupied, or hard to get along with. We all make mistakes, and in a situation that is complicated, there is no right and perfect way to get along.

    Some of the substitute thoughts or self-statements will only be necessary or helpful initially as ways of distracting yourself from persistent urges. You'll have an easier time if you replace the uncomfortable thoughts with other activities. After a while, sobriety will feel less unnatural. Many of the urges will diminish, and you won't need constant replacements.

Group Exercise:

1. Review the following three skills and discuss: (1) Recognize triggers; (2) Monitor triggers; and (3) Strategies for dealing with triggers. See if the group can add to the list or tell stories about their experiences.

2. Make a list of craving triggers. Circle the triggers that you can avoid or to which you can reduce your exposure (like not having alcohol in your home). Discuss as a group what triggers group members

encounter in their communities. For rural clients, their plan may involve asking for help from others. This may be uncomfortable. The therapist should make sure that the group members give and receive support from one another related to asking help from others as part of their plans. As part of their plan, group members also need to describe how they will get help, especially if they have limited access to transportation.

3. Group members identify one high-risk relapse situation that they could encounter soon. Ask each group member how he or she will handle the situation.

4. Develop a craving plan. Pick two or three of the general strategies that were discussed. Ask group members to develop a plan about how they would put their plan into practice if they experienced an urge. (Remember that cravings can come when least expected.) For example: If a distracting activity is selected, which activities would the client pick? Are these activities available now? Which may take some preparation? If the client is feeling craving sensations, who would be best to call? If urge surfing has not been tried before, it might be very helpful to practice before trying it when facing an urge.

5. Check in with the group to see if any client is currently triggered by discussion of cravings and urges. If a client is having difficulty, have the client use the previously discussed skills while in the group so they don't leave the session craving drugs.

6. Distribute Handouts 1 & 2, explaining expectations for completion by next session.

Adapted from Ronald Kadden et al., (1995), Cognitive-Behavioral Coping Skills Therapy Manual. *Rockville, MD: National Institute on Alcohol Abuse and Alcoholism (32–33).*

Skills Session 2—Handout 1: COPING WITH CRAVINGS AND URGES

Reminder Sheet

• Cravings and urges to use are common in recovery. They are not a sign of failure. Learn about craving triggers.

• Urges are like ocean waves. They get stronger only to a point, then they start to go away.

• You win every time you defeat an urge by not using. Urges only get stronger if you give in and feed them. An urge will eventually weaken and die if you do not feed it.

Ways to Cope:

1. Getting involved in a distracting activity.

2. Talking it through with someone.

3. Urge surfing.

Adapted from Ronald Kadden et al., (1995), Cognitive-Behavioral Coping Skills Therapy Manual. *Rockville, MD: National Institute on Alcohol Abuse and Alcoholism (32–33).*

COPING WITH CRAVINGS AND URGES RECORD

Practice Exercise

1. GETTING INVOLVED IN A DISTRACTING ACTIVITY

How many times did you try this skill?   1   2   3   4   5   6

When did you try this skill?   _____

What happened when you tried it?   _____

_____

2. TALKING IT THROUGH WITH SOMEONE

How many times did you try this skill?   1   2   3   4   5   6

When did you try this skill?   _____

What happened when you tried it?   _____

_____

3. URGE SURFING

How many times did you try this skill?   1   2   3   4   5   6

When did you try this skill?   _____

What happened when you tried it?   _____

_____

NOTE: *If you haven't had any cravings and urges since the last session, you may use an example of an urge that you had previously.*

Adapted from Ronald Kadden et al., (1995), Cognitive-Behavioral Coping Skills Therapy Manual. *Rockville, MD: National Institute on Alcohol Abuse and Alcoholism (32–33).*

Skills Session 3: Relaxation

Information for Therapists:

It is important to help clients recognize that there is a difference between participating in diverting and pleasant activities, which distract them from the cares and worries of daily life, and learning how to relax deeply even in difficult situations. Some individuals may find fishing, for example, both deeply enjoyable and relaxing. Such individuals may find the experience of being near the water very positive. Concentrating on the conditions of the water, the habits of the fish, the type of bait most likely to produce results, the best technique for presenting the bait to the fish, and a hundred other considerations that are all part of fishing provide an absorbing distraction from the affairs of daily life. Certainly, someone who finds fishing an enjoyable and relaxing activity should be encouraged to participate in it as part of his overall recovery. However, fishing will not be of any immediate value if that person is involved in a conflict at work and finds himself increasingly agitated, uncomfortable, stressed, and thinking about using a drug. For such situations, clients need to learn how to evoke from within themselves the ability to let go of present feelings of agitation and discomfort and relax.

This social skills session focuses on the second, rather than the first, type of relaxation. The objective is to help clients begin to discover and cultivate in themselves, the ability to relax or at least prevent the acceleration of distress, even in difficult situations. In order to do this, clients must first experience the fact that they have the capacity to relax deeply.

Message to Clients:

People learn to use drugs and alcohol as a way of coping with the stresses of daily life and as a way of letting go of anxiety and worry. People who find relaxation difficult often have trouble with sleep, irritability, concentration, anger, and impulsivity and experience physical problems such as headaches or gastrointestinal problems. People who wish to recover need to learn to relax and let go in ways that do not involve the use of drugs or alcohol. Learning to relax can also improve sleep, health, attitude, and can influence behavior.

There are specific ways that relaxation can be used to help people deal with stress. These include:

- Decreasing tension in specific stressful situations.

- Decreasing tension in general daily stress.

- Decreasing the urge to use drugs or alcohol.

- Increasing ways to think clearly when faced with problems, such as an unexpected crisis or emergency.

At first, practicing relaxation may seem funny, strange, or even uncomfortable, just like learning to ride a bicycle. However, with a little practice it becomes easier. Often, individuals who have used alcohol and drugs for relaxation can achieve surprisingly deep levels of relaxation and pleasant sensation by using their imagination in combination with simple breathing techniques.

Skills:

- Stress can be identified by paying attention to muscular tension.

- Relaxation skills can help in coping with stress, tension, and anxiety.

- Creative imagery can be helpful for relaxation.

- People learn more easily when relaxed.

- Relaxed states are best for reinforcing intentions to not use.

Group members are encouraged to participate in practicing the relaxation techniques presented both in the group sessions and also away from the group, twice a day. It may be helpful to identify times and locations for relaxation prior to leaving this first session. They should record these relaxation appointments on the Practice Exercise sheet.

Each practice session away from the group should end by the client's spending a few minutes imagining a pleasant, relaxing scene and affirming the desire and ability to change positively, especially his or her drug use.

NOTE TO THERAPISTS: *You may use an audiotape especially developed for learning to relax. Background sounds that are familiar to rural individuals, like the sound of a stream or the sound of wind in the trees, could be used, as they are more likely to evoke positive feelings than unfamiliar sounds like the surf.*

While it is important for everyone who is in recovery to be able to relax without using drugs, the relaxation skills presented here may be unfamiliar to many rural clients. Since unfamiliar ideas and people tend to be viewed with caution by those from rural areas (Beltrame, 1979), it might be helpful to begin this activity by asking group members to discuss what they do to relax. For instance, it is likely that answers would include outdoor activities or spending time with close friends or family (Eller, 1997). It might also be helpful to discuss the degree to which these activities can increase relaxation. These activities are to be encouraged as long as they are not associated with drug use, as well as (but not instead of) practicing the relaxation techniques described below.

Finally, it is important that clients feel comfortable during the practice exercises. Some clients may be fine sitting in a chair, others may wish to sit or even lie down on the floor. Each client's decision should be honored. However, it is necessary that clients' backs be reasonably straight to not encumber the diaphragm and allow for free and full breathing. In some cases, clients in very early recovery who are sleep deprived may fall asleep during a relaxation exercise. Therapists should not interpret this as resistance. In fact, it is an indication that the exercise was very helpful to such an individual in lowering their level of agitation to allow sleep.

Group Exercise:

1. Begin by leading a brief discussion about what clients do for relaxation that does not involve the use of alcohol or drugs. Do not be surprised if clients cannot come up with a wide variety of activities. Use the opportunity to point out how much they have relied on chemicals to manage their stress and cope with their daily problems. If there are identified activities that are relaxing and do not involve drug use, encourage clients to do them more often. However, point out to clients that there is a difference between pleasant activities that can lead to a sense of well-being and learning how to relax deeply even in stressful and difficult situations. Discuss the need to learn how to relax, without using drugs, as important in recovery. Also discuss the overall benefits of learning to relax deeply, which can increase the quality of both health and life.

2. Distribute Session 3—Handout 1, a subjective rating scale, to all group members and ask them to estimate their current level of tension. Use something like the following as an introduction:

    "We will now hand out a subjective rating scale to each of you. Estimate and record how tense you feel right now, using the 0–10 scale. '0' being completely and totally relaxed and '10' being as tense as you have ever been in your life. This should only take a moment. When you are done, set the sheet aside. We will talk about the ratings after we finish."

    NOTE TO THERAPISTS: Each group member can pick a number to denote his/her current tension level and record it on a scale on a flip-chart. After the exercise, group members can repeat the procedure to provide a visual aid.

3. Use the taped background of soft music or the seashore, and explain why you are using it. Say something similar to the following:

    "Sometimes it is helpful and pleasant in doing a relaxation exercise to use background sounds that are natural and soothing. All of us tend to associate feelings of peace and relaxation with certain natural sounds like the sound of gentle rain, a babbling brook, or breeze in the trees. Such sounds create a background and remind us of positive and relaxing experiences from our past. I will be using such a tape in our exercise today."

    (Then begin the tape and adjust the volume to a suitable level and, if possible, adjust the lighting to a low level.)

4. Tell clients to get comfortable but to keep their backs straight so that they can breathe easily and deeply. Ask them to let their eyes close gently and to begin to focus on what is going on inside of them, to forget where they are and let themselves begin to relax. Instruct clients to breathe in deeply through their noses, filling their lungs fully; ask them to hold their breath, without strain, for a moment and to exhale through their mouths as if they were gently blowing out a candle. Ask them to repeat the cycle several times, allowing their breathing to fall into a steady and slow rhythm. Use something like the following:

    "Take a moment and get as comfortable as you can. Sit comfortably in a chair or on the floor, or you may even lie down if you wish. Take a moment and find a comfortable position. Just remember to keep your back fairly straight since it is much easier to breathe that way."

(Pause to allow time for clients to get situated.)

"If you're sitting, let your hands rest comfortably on your lap. If you lie down, let your arms rest comfortably at your sides. Now allow your eyes to close gently and begin to withdraw the focus of your awareness from this room and this place, and let it begin to focus inside of you, let it focus on the simple rhythm of your own breathing. Take a moment and let your attention focus on this most basic rhythm of your life."

(Pause for a few seconds.)

"As you focus your attention on the rhythm of your own breathing, notice how it begins to slow and deepen all on its own; it requires no effort on your part whatsoever. Notice how your body becomes looser and more relaxed; it happens all on its own and requires no effort on your part at all. Now, take a slow, deep breath, breathing in through your nose and filling your lungs from the bottom to the top. Hold that breath for just a moment. Now, breathe out through your mouth as if you were gently blowing out a candle. Empty your lungs fully from the top to the bottom. Again, take a slow deep breath, filling your lungs fully from the bottom to the top. Hold the breath, without strain, for just a moment. Now breathe out as if you were gently blowing out a candle. Continue to breathe in that way for a few moments and allow all the tensions of the day to begin to flow out of you. It is almost as if the breath carried the tension out of your body with it. With each breath, you can feel yourself becoming more comfortable and relaxed—a gentle, calm, heavy, almost floating kind of feeling gradually moves through your whole body, increasing just a little bit with every breath that you take. It happens all by itself, naturally, easily, effortlessly; it requires no effort on your part whatsoever."

5. Allow clients about a minute to let their breathing fall into a slow rhythm and to let them get genuinely comfortable. Once you have a sense that this is happening, begin a relaxation script that suggests images to clients that can help them relax and achieve a sense of well-being. The therapist should be mindful of the effect of his/her voice. The voice should be calm and slow, and should, in so far as possible, capture a kind of rhythm in the words. Provide the following information:

"Now, as you continue to sit or lay quietly, breathing slowly and steadily, I'd like you to imagine that you are walking through the woods on a warm, sunny day. Put yourself there, on a path in the middle of the woods, make it real through the unlimited power of your imagination. You are feeling calm, relaxed, at peace, and perfectly secure. Look around you. Look up at the trees above you. Notice how full and green the branches are; how they move gently in the breeze, shifting their patterns of sun and shadow as they move, changing from one shade of green to another in a way that is very soothing, very reassuring."

(Pause)

"Stop for a moment as you take a deep breath and smell the air."

(Pause)

"Notice how it smells of the life of the forest: the slightly spicy smell of ferns, the rich earthy smell of the forest humus, the mixture of a hundred different scents of trees and wildflowers all making a wonderful living perfume. As you walk further, you notice over to one side, a narrow brook running through the woods. It's small, and shallow, and very clear. You can hear the water rippling over the stones on the bottom, making a kind of music. You can see the shifting patterns of sunlight sparkling in the small ripples and eddies caused by the movement of the water over the stones. The sound of the brook is wonderfully enjoyable and calming, and you feel very, very calm and peaceful. Let yourself relax and enjoy your surroundings. . . ."

(Pause)

"As you continue to walk along this path, notice the fallen leaves on the ground. Pick up one of the leaves and hold it in your hand. Rub it between your thumb and finger. Feel the texture of the leaf. Look at it closely. Notice the color. Now let the leaf go . . . let it drop from your hand. Watch it as it flutters slowly to the ground. Continue to walk along feeling very secure, very calm, very much at home."

(Pause)

"As you follow the path you are on, it brings you to a clearing in the middle of the forest. As you get closer, you notice you're standing on the edge of large meadow."

(Pause)

"The meadow is large and level and covered with grass that's sparkles in the sunlight. There are also beautiful wildflowers of every color and description growing among the grasses, and they sway gently in the breeze. As you walk into the meadow, you notice the bright blue sky, you can feel the warmth of the sun, and the movement of the breeze on your skin. It is very, very relaxing."

(Pause)

"As you look to the center of this large meadow, you see there is a small cabin with a front porch. Seated in one of two rockers on that front porch is your best friend. As you walk along a smooth gravel path that leads to the stairs of the porch, you call out a greeting to your friend, who smiles and invites you to sit with him or her. As you sit in the rocker on the front porch of that small cabin in the center of the meadow, you feel perfectly at home—safe and at peace.

(Pause)

"You and your friend begin to talk about things that are important to you, the kind of things that you share when you feel safe in a close friendship. As you talk through that afternoon, you notice that the sky begins to cloud over and it begins to rain very gently. The sound of the rain on the tin roof of the porch makes a wonderful soothing music. You and your friend fall into a companionable silence, sitting quietly, listening to the sound of the warm, gentle rain."

(Pause)

"As you sit comfortably and quietly in the rocker on the front porch of the small cabin in the middle of the beautiful meadow, you begin to feel very warm and drowsy."

(Pause)

"You drift gently into a calm, drowsy sleep and you begin to have a dream about sitting on a rocker next to your best friend on the porch of a small cabin in the middle of the beautiful meadow listening to the rain making music on the roof. And in that dream you feel completely satisfied and completely at peace. There is nothing in the world that you want—nothing that you lack. You are perfectly whole, and complete, and at peace."

(Pause)

"In your dream, you begin to experience a deep sense of gratitude and intense tranquility. This sense grows stronger in you with each breath you take. You know beyond any doubt that if in this moment you desire any good thing for yourself—it is yours. Desire healing and wholeness. Desire recovery and happiness. Desire freedom and serenity. Healing and wholeness. Recovery and happiness. Freedom and serenity. Healing and wholeness. Recovery and happiness. Freedom and serenity.

"As your beautiful dream ends, you feel more fully rested than you have ever felt in your life. You know that the power to heal and be whole, to recover and be happy, to be free and at peace is in you—it is a part of you. You know that you can return to the place of your dream any time you wish by simply taking a deep breath—thinking of the sound of the rain on the roof, or the image of that cabin in the middle of the meadow, or the sensation of the warm breeze on your skin—then breathing out, as if you were gently blowing out a candle."

(Pause)

"Whatever sense of wholeness and gratitude and peace were yours, will be yours again. You can do this anytime you wish, whether in a quiet moment or in the middle of confusion. The wholeness, the gratitude, the peace are inside you—waiting. The place of your dream is waiting and you know the way there and can return at will.

"Now, imagine that you awaken fully, stand up, and wish your friend well and begin to walk down the smooth gravel path that leads to the edge of the woods through the meadow full of grass and wildflowers. Follow the path gradually, past the brook, into the ferns and back to this place—this room. Take a few moments to fully return to this room, in this time, bring with you the sensations you have had and the knowledge you have gained."

(Pause)

"Nothing that you experienced can be taken from you, it is yours, now and always. Come back to this place feeling fully refreshed, completely relaxed, and confident in your ability to meet the challenges that life has in store for you."

6. Give clients a few moments to stretch and get fully back to the group. Ask them to use the Relaxation Rating Scale in Handout 1 to note their current level of relaxation.

   NOTE TO THERAPISTS: You might consider giving the group a brief break and then return to a discussion of clients' experience with the exercise. Do not be surprised to find a range of responses, mostly positive but of varying degrees of strength. Rarely, you may encounter a client who had an adverse response to the exercise and became more anxious as a result. Offer such clients reassurance that that can happen in some cases and that for them use of such an exercise would not be a good idea.

7. Encourage clients to identify times to practice visualization and relaxation and to make a specific commitment to a specific time each day over the next week. You might suggest that some people find it helpful to use a transition time, like when they get home from work. This can serve as a substitute for drug use that sometimes serves a transitional purpose. Or you might suggest that doing an exercise in bed, before sleep, can be helpful. Ask clients to do the practice exercise during the next week, complete Handout 2, and bring it to the group's next session.

8. Once you think that you have allowed for adequate discussion among group members of their experience in the first exercise, make it very clear that whatever positive experience they may have had came from them and not from the exercise. This is a very important point to communicate in this session. The tendency of many chemically dependent individuals is to attribute control over their feelings and actions to some external agent (external locus of control). If you do not challenge this way of thinking, clients will have a sense that the relaxation exercise was a kind of magic, which induced a positive experience. They will come to see relaxation as an experience similar to intoxication: produced by some powerful agent that is outside of their control. As therapist, it is important that you assist clients in understanding that no set of words or images can induce sensations that are not already a part of them. Help clients to understand that the words and images only helped them discover what was already in them. The importance of emphasizing this point and making sure that clients understand and believe it cannot be made strongly enough. Your clients' success in using relaxation to assist them in dealing with difficult situations, especially with their urges and craving, hinges on their willingness to believe that they have the capacity to relax deeply at will. You might begin a discussion of this by asking:

   "How many of you, who had some positive experience during the exercise that we did a while ago, the experience of deep relaxation, is simply a part of you, and how many believe it was a result of the words or sounds to which you listened?"

Respectfully listen to what clients have to say in response to your question. Probe without challenging the thinking that underlies their responses. Depending on whether the clients' responses indicate a belief that the positive experiences are already a part of them or are the result of external circumstances, frame your responses to favor the former. If your clients seem to have difficulty with this notion ask questions like the following:

"Have you ever been in a dangerous situation and acted with courage, or in a difficult situation and acted with intelligence? Where did the courage come from? Where did the intelligence come from? Were the courage or the intelligence a result of the external circumstance or were they a part of you, out of which you responded to the needs of the moment?"

Do everything that you can to impress on clients that when they have a positive experience it is because that positive experience is already a part of them. Also, when they have a negative experience it is because it is a part of them. It is not caused by external things, even though external circumstances may tend to bring out one or the other sort of experience. Take your time in discussing this with clients, and do all that you can to assist them in forming their beliefs in such a way as to empower them to evoke a response of relaxation without the aid of complicated external rituals.

9. Ask clients to think of a situation in which they would feel mildly uncomfortable and tense. Use the rating scale on the work sheet and suggest that it would be a situation in which they would rate their stress as 4 or 5. It could be a situation in which they felt mildly pressured or one in which they had to spend time with someone they did not particularly like. Ask them to make note of the situation on the back of one of the worksheets. Then ask clients to think of a situation in which they felt moderately uncomfortable or stressed, about 6 or 7 on the rating scale. It could be a situation of moderate conflict or one in which they had an important deadline to meet. Ask them to make a note of this second situation on the back of one of the worksheets. Now ask them to think of a situation in which they would feel severe discomfort or stress, an 8 or 9 on the rating scale. It could be a situation of significant interpersonal conflict or one in which they felt overwhelmed by the demands on them. Ask them to make a note of this third situation on the back of one of the worksheets.

10. Lead the next exercise using words like the following (using a background tape with soft music):

"Please sit back comfortably, but keep your back fairly straight. Close your eyes and take a few deep breaths. Begin to let yourself relax a bit and focus the center of your attention on your breathing, on the rhythm of your own breathing. Let your breath come and go easily and naturally."

(Give clients about 15–20 seconds to settle down.)

"Now, imagine yourself back in that meadow in the middle of the forest. Take a deep breath, slowly filling your lungs from the top to the bottom, and as you exhale slowly, emptying your lungs from the bottom to the top, let all the sensations of peace and tranquility, of wholeness and relaxation return to you. Take another deep breath, and let a wave of even deeper relaxation and self-possession wash over you. You really don't have to do anything at all, simply desire it to happen and it happens without any effort on your part whatsoever. Let your breathing slow and deepen, don't force it, just let it happen all by itself. Notice that as this happens you become even more deeply relaxed, and calmer. It's as if these feelings are always there, inside you, waiting to be noticed.

"Now, as you breathe deeply and enjoy whatever feelings of relaxation you are experiencing, I would ask you to think of a word or an image that you associate with your present state. It would be a word like 'peace,' or 'wholeness,' or 'together,' or 'calm.' It could be an image of a tree, or a flower, or an image of yourself, or of some spiritual being. Find a word or an image that seems to fit for you, that really embodies your present state of calm, of wholeness, of peace."

(Pause for 15 or 20 seconds to let clients settle on a word or image.)

"Now, recall to mind the first situation I asked you to identify earlier: the one in which you might feel mildly stressed or uncomfortable. Go ahead, imagine yourself in that situation; make it real with the unlimited power of your imagination."

(Pause for just 10 seconds or so.)

"Now, as you imagine yourself in that situation where you might feel mildly uncomfortable, notice what is happening to your breathing. It is very likely that your breathing has become just a bit more rapid and shallow. Don't try to change or control your breathing, just notice how it changes as you imagine yourself in a situation where you feel slightly uncomfortable or stressed.

(Pause for about 10–15 seconds.)

"Now, I ask you to quite deliberately take a slow, deep breath and allow that word or image you associated with deep relaxation to come to your mind. Notice that some or even all of the feelings of calm begin to return to you almost at once. Notice, too, how your breathing may begin to become slower and deeper. I am going to be quiet for a few minutes so that you can play with that for a while. Imagine yourself in that situation where you feel mildly uncomfortable, let yourself experience that mild discomfort. Then, take a deep breath, call to mind the word or images you have associated with deep relaxation, and let yourself move back into a state of calm and peace. Do that back and forth several times and notice how it becomes easier each time."

(Pause for 2–5 minutes to allow clients to practice.)

"Take a moment to let yourself feel quite relaxed and at ease. Simply let yourself breathe deeply and call to mind that word or image that you associate with feeling relaxed and in control. Now, I would ask you to call to mind the second situation I asked you to identify earlier: the one in which you might feel moderately stressed or uncomfortable. Go ahead, imagine yourself in that situation; make it real with the unlimited power of your imagination."

(Pause for just 10 seconds or so.)

"Now, as you imagine yourself in that situation where you might feel moderately uncomfortable, notice what is happening to your breathing. It is very likely that your breathing is becoming more rapid and shallow. Don't try to change or control your breathing, just notice how it changes as you imagine yourself in a situation where you feel moderately uncomfortable or stressed."

(Pause for about 10–15 seconds.)

"Now, I would ask you to quite deliberately take a slow, deep breath and allow that word or image you associated with deep relaxation to come to your mind. Notice that some or even all of the feelings of calm may begin to return to you almost at once. Notice, too, how your breathing may begin to become gradually slower and deeper. I am going to be quiet for a few minutes so that you can play with that for a while. Imagine yourself in that situation where you feel moderately uncomfortable, let yourself experience that discomfort. Then, take a deep breath, call to mind the word or images you have associated with deep relaxation, and let yourself move back into a state of calm and peace. Do that back and forth several times and notice how it becomes easier each time. Enjoy imagining yourself in a situation where previously you would have felt moderately uncomfortable and stressed, now feeling much calmer and more self-possessed."

(Pause for 2–5 minutes to allow clients to practice.)

"Take a moment to let yourself feel quite relaxed and at ease. Simply let yourself breathe deeply and call to mind that word or image that you associate with feeling relaxed and in control. Now, call to mind the third situation I asked you to identify earlier: the one in which you might feel very stressed or uncomfortable. Go ahead, imagine yourself in that situation; make it real with the unlimited power of your imagination."

(Pause for just 10 seconds or so.)

"Now, as you imagine yourself where you might feel very uncomfortable, notice what is happening to your breathing. It is very likely that your breathing is becoming quite rapid and shallow. Don't try to change or control your breathing, just notice how it changes as you imagine yourself in a situation where you feel very uncomfortable or stressed."

(Pause for about 10–15 seconds.)

"Now, take a slow, deep breath and allow that word or image you associated with deep relaxation to come to your mind. Notice that some or even all of the feelings of calm may begin to return to you almost at once. Notice, too, how your breathing may begin to become gradually slower and deeper. I am going to be quiet for a few minutes so that you can play with that for a while. Imagine yourself in that situation where you feel very uncomfortable, let yourself experience that discomfort. Then, take a deep breath, call to mind the word or images you have associated with deep relaxation, and let yourself move back into a state that is calmer and more peaceful. Do that back and forth several times, and notice how it becomes easier each time. Enjoy imagining yourself in a situation where previously you would have felt very uncomfortable and stressed, now feeling much calmer and more self-possessed."

(Pause for 2–5 minutes to allow clients to practice.)

"Now, forget all about those situations and allow yourself to enjoy a few moments of feeling quite relaxed and at ease. Just breathe deeply and call to mind that word or image that you associate with a state of calm and self-possessed relaxation."

(Pause for 1–2 minutes.)

"Now, make a commitment to yourself that throughout the week you will pay attention, throughout the day to your breathing. Whenever you feel mildly uncomfortable, check to see how you are breathing. If it is becoming shallow and rapid, promise yourself that you will quite deliberately take a deep breath and call to mind the word or images you associate with feeling calm and self-possessed. As you do this, you will allow those feelings of relaxation to come back to you, even in the midst of uncomfortable or difficult situations. Make a commitment to yourself to notice your breathing as you go about your daily activities, doing various things, and being with different people. If you find your breathing becoming rapid or shallow, or you find yourself feeling stressed and uncomfortable, you will take control by taking a deep breath, recalling the word or images you associate with a calm self-possessed state, and allow yourself to actually feel calmer and more self-possessed."

(Pause for 15–20 seconds.)

"Now, take a very deep breath, filling your lungs from the top to the bottom. Exhale, emptying your lungs from the bottom to the top. Gradually open your eyes and stretch, if you would like."

11. Ask clients about their experience with the exercise and discuss them. You may encounter a variety of experiences. Some clients may report that they found it quite easy to move from feeling distressed to some degree to feeling calm. Others may report that they found it very difficult once they were feeling stressed to change it. Assist clients in understanding that being able to relax in difficult situations is a skill. For many years, they have been conditioned to respond in specific ways to specific situations. Make the point that all of them have relied heavily on substances to help them regulate their feelings. Assist clients in understanding that this reliance on substance has aftereffects that are not only psychological in nature but also physical in nature. For example, the use of benzodiazapines (Valium, Xanax, etc.) as a means of dealing with stress over time changes certain structures in the brain. When someone who has relied on such drugs stops using them, the person begins recovery with a brain that is physically more prone to react to events in an anxious fashion. This is not simply a matter of what that person thinks or feels but of very real changes in the structure and function of his/her brain. Fortunately, this problem improves over time as the brain changes to a more normal state. Assist clients in understanding that by doing the kind of things you have taught them in this session they are assisting themselves in returning not just to a state of normalcy but to a state of health.

12. End the group by reviewing upcoming sessions.

Adapted from Monti, P.M. et al. (1989). Treating Alcohol Dependence. *New York: Guilford (89–103).*

Skills Session 3—Handout 1: Relaxation

Relaxation Rating Scale

0	2	5	7	10
No Tension	Very relaxed	Somewhat	Very Tense	Ultimate

Self-Rating *before* relaxation session_____

Self-Rating *after* relaxation session_____

Adapted from Monti, P.M. et al. (1989). Treating Alcohol Dependence. *New York: Guilford (92).*

Skills Session 3—Handout 2: Relaxation

Practice Exercise

Choose something that is a little stressful for you. Before, during, or after the situation, practice using the brief relaxation procedures that you have learned in group—letting go, steady breathing, softly saying a word such as "relax" to yourself.

1. Describe the situation you picked for practicing to relax. Who was there, where was it, and what was happening?

_____

_____

_____

_____

2. What type of relaxation did you personally do?

_____

_____

_____

_____

3. How did it work?

_____

_____

_____

_____

Adapted from Monti, P.M. et al. (1989). Treating Alcohol Dependence. *New York: Guilford (216).*

Skills Session 4: Increasing Pleasant Activities

Information for Therapists:

Developing activities that are pleasant is necessary if a person is to avoid returning to abusing drugs and alcohol. In rural areas work, commitment, and responsibilities are lifestyles and highly valued (Hicks, 1992). Developing pleasant activities may seem difficult. Group members may be uncomfortable taking time for themselves or developing a plan for leisure that does not include family (Looff, 1971; Keefe, 1988). These may be issues that need to be discussed in the group.

In addition, it is possible that pleasant activities are hard for group members to identify because of logistics. In small towns, there may not be ready access to many of the activities that might be available in larger communities. Transportation may not be easily arranged, and lack of finances may make it unreasonable to participate in some activities that group members consider pleasant. It may be helpful to have group members discuss activities they find pleasant within their lifestyle situations.

Message to Clients:

Regular use of alcohol and other drugs consumes so much time and energy that many people who are drug and alcohol dependent, or who abuse substances, feel a void in their lives when they stop using. If a person had a life composed of eating, sleeping, working, and using alcohol and/or drugs, and they stopped using, all that would be left is eating, working, and sleeping. The absence of a "pleasant activity" can be a major problem. For some people, the problem is even more acute since their whole development has involved drugs: all the pleasurable activities in their lives beyond childhood have involved intoxicating substances. These individuals can find it difficult to even conceive of any positive activity that does not involve substance use. Fortunately, with encouragement, practice, and time, individuals can learn to have fun and to enjoy themselves without the use of alcohol and/or drugs. Important things to consider are that this may be problematic at first and that having a specific plan of action is important.

Group Exercise:

1. Talk to clients about the fact that alcohol and drug use occupied a lot of time and energy in their lives and displaced other pleasurable or recreational activities. Point out that the change from using drugs regularly to no use at all is a sudden change, and it can leave a person with a lot of dead time and a real difficulty finding pleasant activities. Deciding on activities that are pleasant, and then making time for them, is the key to renovating life in recovery. You might want to say something like:

   "When you are using alcohol or drugs on a regular basis, using tends to be what you do when you're not sleeping or working—or for some people, what you're doing when you're not sleeping. Using becomes an all-consuming activity in your life. If you decide to stop using and begin recovering, you may find that you have forgotten how to have fun, to enjoy yourself, without drugs. This can be a terrible experience for some people and it drives them right back to using. Even if it isn't a terrible experience, it's hard for most people in early recovery to believe that there is life after drugs. This experience may help to convince you how much alcohol and drug use consumed your life and energy—how much your life was out of balance.

"There are some people in early recovery who try to fill all their new free time and energy with work. That can help for a while but over time it gets old. Those same people can build up resentment or feel that they deserve a reward for all their hard work. Often that reward can be a drink or using a drug. Their lives are out of balance.

"It is important to have a balance of work and play in your life. Research has shown that the number of pleasant activities in which a person engages is directly related to positive feelings [Marlatt & Gordon, 1985]. Similarly, the fewer pleasant activities in which a person engages, the more likely it is that boredom, loneliness, and depression will occur. This research suggests that the more pleasant leisure activities a person has, the more control a person has over their negative feelings. The following activities are presented for you to think about:"

- *Develop a menu of pleasant activities.* The first step in changing your lifestyle is to target pleasant activities that you want to initiate or increase in frequency. One way to do that is to think about/brainstorm a list of activities and pick some that are pleasant for you. People are very different about the types of activities they find pleasant. On the Practice Exercise sheet, write things that you like to do or think you would like doing. Some of the activities may be things you used to enjoy but have not done in a long time. Other things on your menu may be activities you wanted to try but never did.

- *Develop a pleasant-activities plan.* Try scheduling a small block of time each day (30–60 minutes) for pleasant activities. Begin this "personal time" by sitting quietly and mentally reviewing your menu of pleasant activities. You probably will not want to do the same thing every day. One day you may feel the need for relaxation, another day for exercise, and a third day for gardening or music. Schedule some time each day, but do not schedule the activity, so that what you do in your personal time does not become another obligation. Set aside the time, but don't decide on what to do until the time arrives. Then pick from your menu of activities.

"When you think about pleasant activities, recognize that they can be almost anything as long as you enjoy them. A friend of mine told me about a fellow he knows who is an exceptional hunter who spends some time, year around, wandering around in the woods. When he isn't hunting, he is observing the animals he might be hunting at some time. He loves being out in the open in all sorts of weather and he enjoys observing wild things without their knowing. My friend told me that he thought that if this fellow weren't so fond of the taste of wild game, he probably would never waste money on ammunition. Another friend of mine is a devoted fly fisherman. He spends as much time as he can near water. But at least half of the time he isn't fishing, he's just watching and observing what's going on. In the winter, he ties flies for himself and for friends. He spends time reading, especially older books, on fly-fishing. These two people derive a deep satisfaction from what they do. They can hunt or fish alone or with others, so they aren't dependent on anyone else to do what they enjoy. They don't feel that they have anything to prove to anyone or that they have to be the 'best' at what they do, so they can relax and enjoy. Their pleasurable activities lend a real quality to their lives. Others see them as genuinely happy and satisfied people."

2. Ask clients to discuss the patterns that drug and alcohol users can develop and how clients lose the skills of handling leisure time (Lewisohn, Antonuccio, Steinmetz, and Teri, 1984).

3. Ask group members to discuss how well their responsibilities were met as well as their needs to have fun.

4. Ask clients to list activities and to share some of the activities they have listed. Help them to see that someone else's ideas can often stimulate their own thinking and lead to new ideas of what might make for a pleasurable activity.

5. Ask clients to discuss obstacles to pleasant activities.

    •   What feelings are associated with taking time for yourself? *(My Feelings)*

    •   What pressures do you have on you if you take time for yourself? *(Pressures on Me)*

    •   How will other people in your life respond? *(Others' Actions)*

    •   What can I do to follow through with taking care of myself? *(My Actions)*

    NOTE TO THERAPISTS: *This is an introduction to the thought mapping principles used throughout the rest of the manual.*

6. Also ask clients to share their commitments about providing time for themselves on a regular basis. What are they willing to commit to doing in the following week?

Adapted from Monti, P.M. et al. (1989). Treating Alcohol Dependence. *New York: Guilford Press (87-89).*

Skills Session 4—Handout 1: INCREASING PLEASANT ACTIVITIES

Reminder Sheet

- Develop a list of pleasant activities.

  Some examples would be: Watching TV, camping, boating, fishing, attending sporting events, walking, hiking in the woods, hunting, rock climbing, taking a nap, doing craft or art work, being with friends, photography, singing, dancing, going to church functions, puzzles, listening to the radio, being with animals, sitting in the sun, gardening, telling jokes, visiting friends, writing letters, collecting things, sewing, shopping, bird watching, reading, traveling, people watching, playing cards, being with children, repairing things, cooking, and star gazing.

- "Pleasant activities" are activities that have some physical, mental, or spiritual value.

- Plan "pleasant activity" time at least three times each week.

- The goal is to achieve balance between the things that you should do and the things that you want to do, so that you feel satisfied with your daily life.

- The more fun things you do, the less you will miss drugs and alcohol, and the less likely you will be to use drugs or alcohol to create fun in your life.

Adapted from Monti, P.M. et al. (1989). Treating Alcohol Dependence. *New York: Guilford Press (213).*

Skills Session 4—Handout 2: INCREASING PLEASANT ACTIVITIES

Practice Exercise

- Write down at least three "pleasant activities" that you enjoy doing.

_____

_____

_____

- Schedule "pleasant activities" three times every week for these things. Select the activity from the list that you made.

After completing your "pleasant activity" for the week, write it down.

FIRST ACTIVITY_____

When_____

Where_____

SECOND ACTIVITY_____

When_____

Where_____

THIRD ACTIVITY_____

When_____

Where_____

Skills Session 5: Problem Solving

Information for Therapists:

In rural areas, where people usually value independence and self-sufficiency (Beltrame, 1978) there may be reluctance to talk about problems, especially with persons outside the family. Talking about problems in a treatment group may feel like betraying their family for some. Clients may struggle with fatalism—the strong belief that problems should be endured because they cannot be solved (Eller, 1996). This has resulted from years of financial and social exploitation of the Appalachian region, as well as the lack of political and economic power to address social problems (Gaventa, 1980). Therefore, group members may place more emphasis on coping with problems rather than solving problems.

The therapist needs to understand these powerful cultural messages so that they can be used as part of the group discussion. The therapist needs to be patient, since such beliefs are very strong and often take time to change.

Rural clients struggle with many serious problems including poverty, unemployment, financial stress, illness, and lack of access to transportation. Sometimes in rural areas there are few recovery resources for clients, and group members might have little access to support groups and other needed services. These situations should be discussed during case management sessions, but they also can be the practical focus for this problem-solving session.

Message to Clients:

People in recovery from drug and alcohol abuse often have problems that need attention. During many years of drug or alcohol use, they have developed poor problem-solving habits, and some have never learned effective approaches to problem solving. It takes time and attention and practice to change patterns of living that may have built up over months and years of making poor decisions. The drug or alcohol dependent person will most likely need help in learning or relearning how to make good decisions and solve problems.

Drug- or alcohol-dependent persons often procrastinate and avoid problem solving. Problems seem overwhelming. The dependent individual may rely on substance use as the means of coping with life's problems. Further, drug- and alcohol-using persons may misattribute their problems, believing that they are caused by someone else's actions. When this happens, they may passively expect others to solve problems for them.

Procrastinating, relying on continued drug use, or expecting others to solve problems causes more problems for the drug and alcohol user. Difficult problems become catastrophes if we do not have strategies to deal with them. For instance, not paying a traffic ticket or not paying child support, can result in warrants or arrests that did not need to happen had the person paid attention to the problem in earlier stages and taken responsibility for a solution. Some clients suffer from the opposite problem—they move far too quickly to deal with problems. Impulsive people act rashly before thinking. The consequences of this problem-solving style can also be catastrophic.

Unnecessary emotional stress threatens recovery. Unmanaged stress is often followed by a slip or relapse to drug or alcohol use. Helping a person a) assess problems and solutions, b) decide on a course of action, c) follow through with the action, and d) evaluate the results, can be a very significant aid to recovery. Building this skill takes attention and practice, but is a rewarding discipline, as self-esteem develops from solving problems successfully.

Skills:

Elements of problem-solving usually include the following:

1. Recognizing a problem.

   • What cues a person to the problem?

      —Body cues (indigestion, craving)

      —Thought and feelings cues (anxiety, depression, or loneliness)

      —Behavior cues (meeting standards at work, being with family and/or friends)

      —Reactions to others cues (anger, lack of interest, withdrawal)

      —Cues from others (avoidance/criticism)

2. Problem identification.

   • What is the specific problem?

3. Considering various approaches (Bedell, Archer & Marlowe, 1980).

   • What can I do about the problem?

      —Brainstorm.

      —Change my point of view or frame of reference.

      —Adapt a solution that has worked before.

4. Selecting the most promising approach.

   • What will happen if.... (think ahead)

5. Assessing the effectiveness of the solution.

   • How did it work?

Problems cannot be avoided—they are part of everyday life! They are often a result of how we interact with or avoid others. Solving a problem involves paying attention to others to assess the situation. The situation only becomes a problem when there is no solution.

Often, our thoughts and feelings can affect problems. Drug and alcohol users often make decisions impulsively or delay making decisions. Acting impulsively, without thinking, is not usually an effective way to solve problems. Doing nothing is not effective either. Problems build up over time, and can produce negative feelings—like fear and anxiety. Problems that are not dealt with can lead to a bad outcome, which can lead to relapse.

Effective problem solving involves:

- Problem recognition.

- Problem identification.

- Consideration of various solutions.

- Selecting the best alternatives.

- Assessing the effectiveness of the solution.

At the end of this session, each group member should be able to do the following:

—*Recognize Problems:* Understanding that particular behaviors in their lives are the sources of discomfort and distress.

—*Delay Action, and Think:* Slowing down before responding can lead to more adaptive coping.

—*Identify Problems:* Being able to specify those circumstances, feelings, and values that contribute to problematic behaviors.

—*Consider Various Solutions:* Identifying the options available for behavior in a problem situation.

—*Select the Best Alternative:* Making a choice of action based on a rational projection of probable outcome.

—*Assess the Effectiveness of a Solution:* Setting criteria to determine whether a specific behavior has been a successful solution.

Group Exercise:

1. Introduce problem solving using the material contained in the message section of this session. List the skills and key points on a flip-chart and discuss.

2. As the group begins to acknowledge the need to address problems, introduce thought mapping as

an effective way to do this, by saying:

> "To guide and help our discussion of problem solving, we are going to use a method called thought mapping. This is a way of focusing our discussion so that we can see how one thing relates to another. Using mapping is especially helpful when we are trying to understand what kinds of things affect our problems and what kinds of things we can do to solve problems. For starters, we will be using a blank form to guide our discussion of identifying problems."

3. Put the following blank map on a flip-chart or blackboard—or have it copied before the group session for each group member.

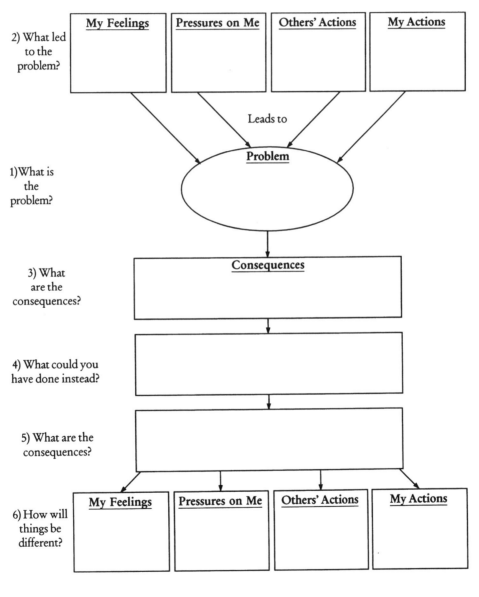

4. Briefly explain the parts of the map.

    —*Problem:* The behavior that is identified as a problem.

    —*What led to the problem:* The feelings, actions of the client and others, as well as the pressures felt by the client that are identified as leading up to the behavior identified as a problem.

    —*Consequences:* The outcome of the problem behavior.

    —*What could have been done instead:* Alternative behavior.

    —*How will things be different:* The feelings, pressures, actions of others, and actions of self if the alternative is chosen.

5. Using thought mapping, demonstrate how mapping can be used to analyze the story. The therapist should tell a story to "prime the pump" and then map the problem embedded in that story. Emphasize the various responses or solutions. Have the group discuss these responses and solutions.

    "Recently, a client told me this story: 'I couldn't believe the time my wife had me thrown in jail. I had been out of work for a few weeks—the factory had laid most of us off after we lost a strike. Like every other guy who was laid off, I went out looking for work and had no luck. When I got home, no supper, and no wife. About an hour later she comes in, smelling of alcohol. Things hadn't been good before I was laid off, and it was a lot worse after. I hollered at her for being gone and asked where the hell she had been and who she was with. She laughed and told me where to go. I told her she was my wife and she damn well better tell me. She said she didn't have to tell me anything since I was not much of a man anyhow, having to depend on a woman to pay the rent. I hauled off and hit her in the shoulder. She came back at me and hit me back. Then I busted her mouth. She started screaming and crying. She was really bleeding then. I left and went to my buddy's trailer up the holler. Next thing I know, the deputies were there, hauling my butt to jail. My father heard about what happened and bailed me out. By God, the next day I started smoking again.'

    "This story could be mapped in the following way:"

    (Refer to map on following page.)

6. Ask group members to complete the map by answering the remaining questions. Let the group know that it is often best to think of the map as having two parts: questions 1–3 are for problem identification and questions 4–7 are for problem solution. Then ask if a group member is willing to talk about a specific problem behavior from their recent past. Lead a discussion about that problem behavior, filling in the various parts of the map as a guide.

7. Ask the group to complete problem identification (questions 1–3) maps for at least two problems that they individually have experienced in the recent past.

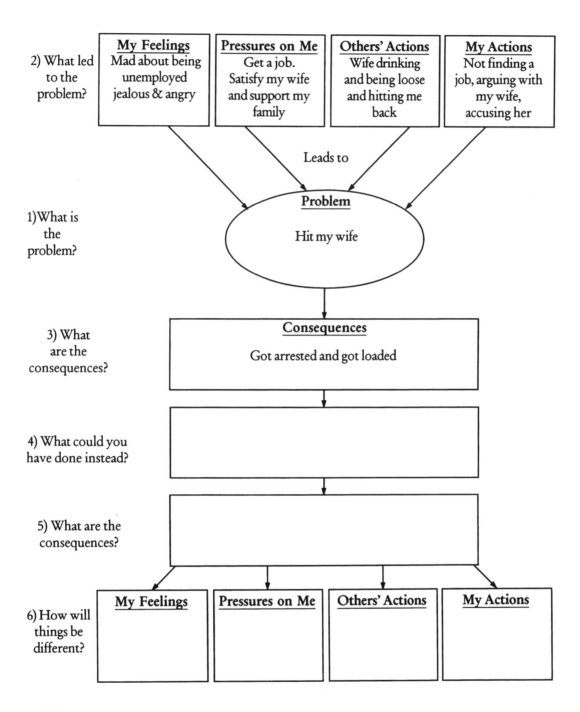

2) What led to the problem?

My Feelings	Pressures on Me	Others' Actions	My Actions
Mad about being unemployed jealous & angry	Get a job. Satisfy my wife and support my family	Wife drinking and being loose and hitting me back	Not finding a job, arguing with my wife, accusing her

Leads to

1) What is the problem?

Problem

Hit my wife

3) What are the consequences?

Consequences

Got arrested and got loaded

4) What could you have done instead?

5) What are the consequences?

6) How will things be different?

My Feelings	Pressures on Me	Others' Actions	My Actions

7) What can you do now?

8. Ask the group to select one of the problems they have identified as a problem to which they can explore solutions (questions 4–7) by using the map format.

9. Distribute Handouts 1 & 2 and explain the expectation that each group member complete a map by the next group session.

NOTE TO THERAPISTS: *When working through the map format, use the group process to identify options for resolving the problem. Invite group members who are facing similar problems to identify factors that have led to and contribute to the problem. Also, take time to discuss successful solutions to these problems. Assist group members in selecting measures of change that are realistic and obtainable.*

Make sure that enough time is allowed to reinforce the process. Point out to group members that a problem analysis is important prior to exploring problem solutions. Emphasize the fact that there are usually several possible responses to any problem situation and that they will have different outcomes. Make sure that group members are aware that a small investment in problem solving can avoid the needless waste of time, money, and relationships.

Skills Session 5—Handout 1: PROBLEM SOLVING

Reminder Sheet

Problem solving includes the following steps for solving a problem:

1. *Recognize that a problem exists.* "Is there a problem?"

   We get clues from our bodies, our thoughts and feelings, our behavior, our reactions to other people, and the ways that other people react to us.

2. *Identify the problem.* "What is the problem?"

   Describe the problem as accurately as you can. Break it down into manageable parts.

3. *Consider various approaches to solving the problem.* "What can I do?"

   —Brainstorm to think of as many solutions as you can.

   —Try taking a different point of view.

   —Try to think of solutions that worked before.

   —Ask other people what worked for them in similar situations.

4. *Select the most promising approach.* "What will happen if...?"

   Consider all the positive and negative aspects of each possible solution, and select the one likely to solve the problem with the least hassle.

5. *Look at how good the solution to the problem is.* "How did it work?"

   After you have given it a fair trial, does it seem to be working out? If not, consider what you can do to beef up the plan, give it up, or try another possible solution.

Skills Session 5—Handout 2: PROBLEM SOLVING

Practice Exercise
Select a situation with which you expect to have "difficulty coping." Describe the situation. Make a list of antecedents (things that led up to the situation): My Feelings, Pressures on Me, Others' Actions, and My Actions. Look at possible solutions and note your favorite.

1. Identify the situation:

_____

_____

2. What were your actions leading up to the situation?

_____

_____

3. What were your feelings leading up to the situation?

_____

_____

4. What pressures did you have on you?

_____

_____

5. What were the actions of other people that led to this situation?

_____

_____

6. What are some of the solutions to the situation?

_____

_____

_____

_____

_____

_____

_____

_____

Skills Session 6: Awareness and Management of Negative Thinking

Information for Therapists:

The therapist needs to emphasize that recovering persons are especially vulnerable to becoming overwhelmed by negative and distorted thoughts that can evoke strong negative moods such as anger, depression, and anxiety. Since many persons use drugs and alcohol to manage such emotions, it becomes important to prevent thinking and feeling from spiraling out of control. Recent research indicates that many recovering persons suffer from residual neurocognitive deficits that can compromise accurate perception and information processing (thinking). Learning to link events, thoughts, and feelings is an important corrective to relying on such distorted perceiving and thinking.

Message to Clients:

The way we think influences how we feel. When we fall into habitual and automatic patterns of negative thinking, we tend to develop habitual patterns of negative feeling. Negative thinking can be a kind of self-fulfilling prophecy that leads to a lot of painful experiences in our lives. Working on changing our thinking does not usually bring immediate results, but in the long run it can change our lives for the better. If we are willing to change our patterns of negative thinking, which does much to color our mood, we can, over time, feel much less anxious, depressed, and frustrated. Negative thinking also blocks the ability to realistically perceive and respond to situations and other people. Replacing negative thinking with more hopeful thinking can empower persons to actively and productively address the challenges they face.

Skills:

Catching your Negative Thinking

- Recognizing General Patterns of Negative Thinking

- Categories of Negative Thinking (Ellis, 1975)

    —Unrealistic Goals

    —Catastrophizing

    —Overgeneralization

    —Expecting the Worst

    —Self-Putdowns

    —All-or-Nothing Thinking

Stopping your Negative Thinking

- Substitute Positive for Negative "self-talk"

- Takes practice and repetition

- Gradually helps with moodiness, depression, anger, tension, and self-esteem

- People or events cannot change your mind unless you let them

- You have total control of what you think or say to yourself

Group Exercise:

1. Use the following story to evoke personal stories from the group:

Prime the Pump:

"Carl has just stopped drinking and begun to attend AA and counseling. His family was not very supportive of this move, especially his alcoholic father, who saw Carl 'acting like he was better than the rest of the family.' Carl has always had a very difficult relationship with his father, who constantly criticized him when he was a child and a teenager.

"Carl hadn't had a drink or smoked pot in a month. One morning he arrived at work and found a note on his locker from his boss that said, 'Please see me tomorrow at the start of your shift.' Carl quickly put the note in his pocket and began to work on the line. He began to sweat and feel nauseous. He could hardly handle lifting and inspecting the wheels because he felt so ill. He let two flawed wheels go down the line and the foreman came over and asked him what was wrong since Carl usually had 100 percent error-free shifts. 'I don't know what's wrong.'

"After his shift Carl stopped at the grocery to pick up some milk. He passed the wine and beer shelves and put a six-pack in his grocery cart. He wheeled it to the counter and as the cashier began to ring up his items, he took the beer out and set it in an empty cart. He went home, and his girlfriend was cooking supper. As they talked, he emptied his pants to find the grocery receipt and the change, and discovered the note from his boss and read it again.

"Carl's girlfriend asked him what was wrong. He showed her the note and said that he had better start looking for another job because if the boss wanted to see him, he was probably going to get fired. 'They never want to talk with you unless you're in trouble.' His girlfriend tried to tell him that it might be something else, but Carl got upset and told her he didn't want to talk about it. That night Carl had trouble sleeping. He wished he had brought that six-pack home. He looked around to see if he could find any weed that he forgot to get rid of, but he couldn't—He and his girlfriend had really cleaned the house. He began to worry about where he would live if he were fired. He figured that his girlfriend would dump him if he didn't have a job. He turned on the TV and finally fell asleep.

"The next day when he went to work he walked to the management area of the plant. His boss saw him coming and motioned him over to his office. 'You look tired, Carl,' he said. Then his boss asked him if he was interested in filling in as foreman while the regular guy was on vacation."

2. Ask the group to discuss their response to this story. Especially focus on the relationship between the event (receiving the boss's note), Carl's thinking, and his feelings. An important point is the fact that Carl had strong feelings before becoming aware of his negative thinking about the note. Many clients will experience feelings and act on them without linking them to thoughts or events. Using this story, the therapist can model this type of careful analysis. Group members might find this confusing or ponderous at first, and the therapist should proceed patiently as the group begins to understand the connections.

3. The therapist can draw this simple diagram on a flip-chart and discuss:

$$A \longrightarrow B \longrightarrow C$$

Antecedent   Behavior   Consequences

4. Help the group to use personal experiences to discuss events in their lives about which they have negative thoughts and feelings. Talk about what they felt negatively about, and examine thoughts and feelings that resulted. Group members can support one another in strategies to recognize and stop negative thinking. The therapist should be supportive by suggesting ways to change negative thinking or to encourage group members to talk about a situation where they or someone close to them was able to successfully change thinking and eventually—their behavior.

5. Assist group members in identifying one past event that led to strong negative feelings and to drug use. The therapist and the group then analyze the thought process that came between the event and the feeling. Group members are asked to identify thoughts that accompany negative feelings that they experience over the next few days.

6. Describe the method of thought mapping using the following:

"To guide and help our discussion about negative thinking, we are going to use a method called thought mapping. This is a way of focusing our discussion so that we can see how one thing relates to another. Using this approach is especially helpful when we are trying to understand what kinds of things affect us negatively and what kinds of things we can do to change them. To start, we will use a blank form to guide our discussion of negative thinking."

Put the following blank map on a flip-chart or blackboard:

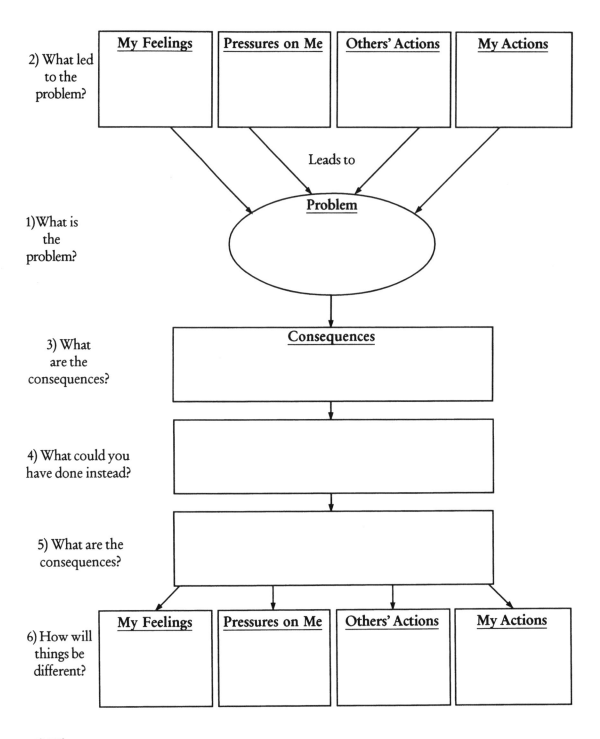

2) What led to the problem?

My Feelings

Pressures on Me

Others' Actions

My Actions

Leads to

1) What is the problem?

Problem

3) What are the consequences?

Consequences

4) What could you have done instead?

5) What are the consequences?

6) How will things be different?

My Feelings

Pressures on Me

Others' Actions

My Actions

7) What can you do now?

7. Ask each group member to think of some event or situation in the recent past that evoked bad feelings and which led or almost led to drug use. Give the group a minute or two to do this.

8. Ask any group member who is willing, to take the lead in sharing his experience with the group. Write a summary of the situation or event in the appropriate box on the map. Ask that individual if he can recall the kinds of thoughts that he had when he was confronting that situation or event. If the person has difficulty doing this, ask what kinds of thoughts he has as he thinks about the situation or event now. Ask other group members to help by suggesting what they might think in a similar situation.

   NOTE TO THERAPISTS: List the thoughts that come from this discussion in the appropriate box on the map. Try to get as complete a list as is possible. Ask the group member to recall the feelings and emotions that arose from the situation or event and his thoughts. Point out that an event or situation is considered uncomfortable mainly because of the feelings that surround it. Try to get as specific expression of the feeling(s) as possible.

   Then ask the client what behaviors resulted from the chain of events/situation, thinking, and feelings. Since you asked for situations related to drug use, that behavior will be listed. Ask about any other behaviors that were also an outcome of the process.

9. Ask group members whether there are other situations or events that produce similar thoughts, feeling, and behaviors, and note that people tend to feel uncomfortable in similar situations. In addition, chemically dependent individuals may have some special difficulty with situations of interpersonal conflict (Marlatt & Gordon, 1980, 1985).

10. Ask the group whether they can imagine a different set of thoughts, in the same situation(s) giving rise to a different set of feelings and a different set of behaviors.

   Record the alternative thoughts and alternative feelings together with alternative behaviors in the appropriate boxes on the map.

11. Point out that if the group members could begin to change thought patterns in an uncomfortable situation or when confronted with an uncomfortable event, they could improve the probability of having a better behavioral outcome.

12. If time allows, ask for another uncomfortable situation from the group and discuss it.

   Lead a group discussion on what group members might do when they find themselves in an unpleasant or uncomfortable situation to stop the flow of negative thinking and/or substitute more positive alternative thinking.

   If the group has difficulty coming up with ways of interrupting or changing negative thinking, put yourself into the role of a group member in one of the situations, beset by negative thoughts, and ask the group to advise you. Note that individuals are sometimes more able to give good advise to others rather than to themselves.

13. Write the suggestions that emerge from the discussion on the board or on a flip-chart. Only if the group is completely stuck, offer the following suggestions:

- Count to 10, take a deep breath, and ask yourself how else you can see what's happening or think of what is OK in your life. Replace your thoughts about what you can't do with what you can do.

- Turn it over, Let go and let God, Easy does it. Ask yourself, "What's the worst that can really happen?"

- Reassure yourself that it will be fine in the long run, even though things are pretty tense right now. Or even if I made a mistake, I can correct it and learn.

14. Distribute Handout 1 and discuss.

15. Distribute Handout 2 and ask group members to complete it by the next session.

16. Ask group members to think of one uncomfortable situation they are likely to encounter in the next week and decide how they will go about changing their thinking so that they can feel better and have a better outcome.

Skills Session 6—Handout 1: CHANGING NEGATIVE THINKING

Reminder Sheet

Recall the Good in People and Situations:

- Concentrate on what went well in a situation rather than what went badly.

- Concentrate on what is good about you rather than what is bad.

Challenge Irrational Beliefs and Unrealistic Expectations:

- Avoid extreme words:
  —Should, must, ought to, have to
  —Awful, terrible, disastrous
  —Always, never, forever

Decatastrophizing:

- Catastrophic thoughts can be countered by:
  —Asking what the probability is of this occurring.
  —Asking what would keep it from occurring, or if it could be changed.
  —Asking what it would take to accept it.

Relabeling the Distress:

- Tell yourself the feelings are a signal to practice new skills, not to use again.

Blaming the Event, Not Yourself:

- Making a mistake is human—practice acceptance.

Reminding Yourself to Stay "On Task":

- Focus on what needs to be done.

- Don't think about being upset.

- Use your energy to get the job done.

Hopefulness Statements:

- "I can change how I respond to her."

- "It'll be okay in the long run, even though it's difficult now."

Self-Reinforcement:

- Don't forget to reward (not with using!) yourself with a pat on the back when you handle a difficult situation well.

Skills Session 6—Handout 2: CHANGING NEGATIVE THINKING

Practice Exercise

GIVE A PERSONAL EXAMPLE FOR EACH OF THE FOLLOWING:

1. *Unrealistic Goals:* "I must, should, have to do everything right"' or "Other people should always be reliable, trustworthy, friendly, on time."

    _____

2. *Catastrophizing:* "If things don't work out the way I expect, then it's useless, awful, terrible, the end of the world."

    _____

3. *Overgeneralization:* "I'm never on time," "I am always depressed."

    _____

4. *Expecting the Worst:* "I will never get my act together," "This marriage is doomed to fail," or "I know nobody really cares about me."

    _____

5. *Self-Putdowns:* "I don't deserve better," "I am stupid, unreliable, weak," "My dad always said I was no good."

    _____

6. *"All-or-Nothing Thinking":* "If I am ever late for work at all, then I will get fired and never get another job as long as I live," "If people don't totally love me, then they must hate me," "Either I am all good or I am all bad."

    _____

Adapted from Ellis, A. (1975). The New Guide to Rational Living. *New York: Harper & Row.*

Skills Session 7: Anger Awareness and Management

Information for Therapists:

Dealing with anger effectively may be more difficult in rural communities. Traditional attitudes of stoicism and keeping problems to oneself are common in rural Appalachian families (Keefe, 1988; Eller, 1997). Fatalistic and pessimistic beliefs among rural people dictate that they can only make a little difference (Keefe, 1988; Looff, 1971). While such self-control is prized—especially among males—repressing anger when the stress of controlling anger becomes too great can lead to aggression (Keefe, 1988).

Message to Clients:

Many people who relapse report that they first slipped during a moment of anger. Anger is a "normal feeling," which is usually a response to events and people who frighten or threaten. The recovering drug and alcohol abuser must be careful when he/she experiences anger. *While anger itself is neither good nor bad, how a person acts when he/she is angry can be constructive or destructive.* Those who don't respond well to anger may become more impulsive and make poor decisions.

Skills:

- *Becoming aware of situations which trigger anger*

  There is a difference between feeling anger and acting on anger. Behaving angrily, acting aggressively, impulsively, passively, or passive-aggressively can have negative consequences.

  Anger is neither good nor bad, but is an intense feeling, and depending on our reactions to it, can be either constructive or destructive.

  Destructive anger can lead to:

  —Impulsive actions

  —Poor decision-making

  —Inhibiting communication

  —Masking other feelings

  —Creating emotional distance

  —Triggering hostility in others

Constructive anger can lead to:

—Signals that there is a problem

—Energizing a person to take action

—Increasing personal power

—Helping communicate negative feelings

—Changing destructive relationships

—Helping to avoid misunderstandings

—Helping to strengthen relationships

- *Becoming aware of internal reactions to anger*

  —*Feelings:* Frustration, irritation, feeling wound up or on edge often come before anger, and can be handled before it builds up.

  —*Physical reactions:* Muscle tension, headaches, sweating, rapid breathing, jaw clenching, pounding heart, sweating.

  —*Difficulty falling asleep:* May be due to angry thoughts and feelings not addressed.

  —*Feeling tired, helpless, or even depressed.* For example, past coping with anger has been ineffective. Sometimes even trying to change what was happening has not worked.

- *Learning to calm down when angry*

  - Slow down

  - Relax and take a deep breath

  - Count to 10

  - Decide on a phrase to use for yourself when angry—"chill out," "cool it!"

  - Do something physical (i.e., walk, lift weights, etc.)

- *Identifying the source of anger*

  - "What's really got me ticked?"

- • "What can I do?"

- • "What part of my body is responding?"

- • *Reviewing options*

  - • "What's in my best interest here?"

  - • "If I do _____, they might do _____."

- • *Problem resolution*

  - • Select a good thing to do after thinking about it for a while.

  - • Talk with someone to help.

Group Exercise:

1. Present an introduction of the topic using the material contained in the skills section of this session. List skills on a flip-chart and discuss.

2. Present the following story to provide an example of how things that come before influence behaviors and later consequences for "ABC Approach" and thought mapping:

Prime the Pump:

"I almost got fired the other day. And it was my son Junior's fault. I let him borrow my car. Now the boy doesn't have insurance, and even though he's got a job, he doesn't pay for his own insurance. His mother would let him do anything, even though he treats her like dirt except when he needs something. So I hear all of this crap. I ask him where he's going. He says he's looking for a new job—one that pays more. So I let him take the car. I should have known he lied to me. He heads straight to his girlfriend's to pick her up, and they go to a party. Except they never get there because he has a wreck. He says some boy was drunk and pulled out in front of him. Except nobody knows the truth since he never gets a damn police report! Anyway he calls, and I go get him in the truck. I see the wreck. Just looking at it I see $800 in bodywork. I start screaming at him, especially when I see the girl and figure out where he really went! All the way home we're shouting. He starts cussing, and I cuss him back. When we get home he's cussing me in the driveway. His mother runs out and tells me to back down. I start screaming at her for taking up for him again. By now I'm so damn mad I can't think straight. I can't stop.

"I just want to haul off and beat him up. My littlest daughter runs back into the house crying. I feel bad about that. Every damn one of them took his side. I left that night and went out and got so drunk I didn't show up for work the next morning. The whole family is mad as hell at me. My wife won't speak to me and neither will my boy. Three weeks of this! My boss asks me every night if I'm planning to show up the next morning!"

3. Describe thought mapping as follows:

    "To guide and help our discussion of anger management, we are going to use a method called thought mapping. This is a way of putting our discussion together so that we can see how one thing relates to another. Mapping is especially helpful when we are trying to understand what kinds of things affect our feelings and what kinds of things we can do to change them."

    Put the following map on a flip-chart or blackboard and pass out copies.

4. Ask the group to assist you in completing the map by providing possible answers to questions 4-7.

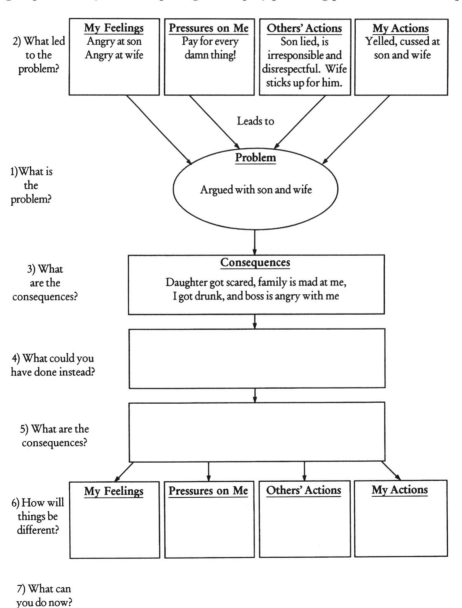

5.   Additionally, we can apply the ABC approach to how anger is generated in this manner:

ANTECEDENTS	BEHAVIORS	CONSEQUENCES
	(what happens)	(what comes after)
(what comes before)		
Risk state detonated by a "trigger" event.	Person: thinks angrily/calmly feels anger/calm behaves rationally/irrationally	Others: comply avoid fight back, etc.

Here is an example of how ABC works in a destructive way:

A parent has long-term resentment about his son's irresponsible behaviors. Son wrecks the car.	Parent: Thinks—"He's no good, he has screwed me over again." Feels—enraged Behaves—screams, shouts, at son and family	Others: Son withdraws. Spouse angry. Daughter scared. All family withdraw from contact with him. Parent gets drunk.

Here is an example of how ABC works in a constructive way:

A parent is frustrated with son's irresponsible behavior, but realizes he has contributed to its development. Son wrecks the car.	Parent: Thinks—"This is a disaster, I need to manage this situation maturely." Feels—angry but in control Behaves—Takes some time out; Calls a family meeting; talks about situation with everyone; develops appropriate plan of action to discipline son and get car paid for.	Parent remains calm and in control. Gets support from family. Son is pressured by everyone to take responsibility and pay for the car. Parent sees self as a competent parent.

6. Ask if a group member is willing to discuss a time when they felt or acted angry recently. Lead a discussion focused on that "anger event," filling in the thought map as a guide.

7. Complete anger identification maps for an anger event presented by the group—one using effective skills and one using ineffective skills. Use the example as a guide to facilitate group discussion.

> *NOTE TO THERAPISTS:* When describing the approach, use the group process to identify options in responding to events that trigger anger. Invite group members who are facing or who have faced similar problems to disclose to the group, citing the factors that led and contributed to destructive or constructive expressions of anger. Also assist group members to select measures of change, which are realistic and obtainable.
>
> Make sure that enough time is allowed to reinforce the process. Point out that a problem analysis is important prior to exploring problem solutions. Emphasize the fact that there are usually several possible responses to any anger-producing situation and that they will have different outcomes. Make sure that group members are aware of the fact that a small investment in coping with anger-producing situations can avoid the needless loss of time, money, and relationships.
>
> The therapist also needs to keep in mind that this group session might be the first time some group members have been given permission to examine their anger. Some members might find it a "safe" place to disclose the roots of their anger by revealing experiences of childhood and/or adult trauma. For example, women who are, or who have been, victims of domestic violence might begin to discuss their experiences. Others might link their drinking and drugging behavior with childhood sexual abuse and want to talk about those experiences. People who have "stuffed" their emotions for so long often feel a need to release "all" of their history at once. Because of their previous experiences, they may be unable to understand that the group setting is probably not the best place. This kind of disclosure—while at first cathartic for the person—might prove troubling for other group members or even for the therapist.
>
> It is crucial that the therapist be prepared to validate persons "working through" their anger while not allowing their stories to "swallow up" the group session. In other words, the therapist needs to empathize and support these members but not allow the group to become a psychotherapy group or even an individual session within the group. This is important for the long-term stability of the trauma survivor as well. Persons who have not been assisted in limiting or "pacing" their disclosures can become psychologically disorganized or feel they have "stripped" themselves (Briere, 1992). This is even more likely if the person begins disclosing in a group setting. While a member might be resentful when the group therapist "slows" them down in such disclosures, they will probably be glad later that this process was targeted during individual sessions in a manner that respects the complexity of post-traumatic experience.
>
> It is important that any person who presents this kind of experience should be followed individually. Some states have laws that demand reporting if the abuse is current and continuing in clients' lives. Consult your state regulations regarding reporting.

8. Distribute Handout 1 and discuss.

Skills Session 7—Handout 1: ANGER AWARENESS AND MANAGEMENT

Reminder Sheet

Becoming angry can result from:

$$A \longrightarrow B \longrightarrow C$$

A	B	C
Antecedent	**Behavior**	**Consequences**

Anger can result from the long-term situations we are in being "triggered" by a negative event. How a person thinks about what has happened influences how they feel and then how they behave. If the behavior is rational and in control, the consequences will probably be positive and helpful to the angry person. *Remember, it is possible to be angry, but still respond constructively!* If the angry person behaves in an irrational, aggressive manner, then it is likely that others will "punish" or "withdraw" from the angry person. Things can get even worse!

ANTECEDENT	BEHAVIOR	CONSEQUENCES
(what comes before)	(what happens)	(what comes after)
Long-term "risk state" triggered by a negative event.	Person feels angry but thinks of ways to control anger & act responsibly.	Person stays in control & accomplishes what needs to be done.

Skills Session 8: Interpersonal Violence

Information for Therapists:

The United States leads the industrialized world in rates of homicide. Researchers are puzzled by the escalating rates of lethal violence in the U.S., especially among males between 16–24 years old. Three causes, being investigated, include the availability and misuse of firearms, the increased violence associated with the illegal drug trade, and the greater willingness of contemporary adolescents and adults to use lethal violence (Potter & Mercy, 1997).

One line of research that pertains to rural people in the southern parts of the United States such as Kentucky is the contention that southern culture has high standards of personal honor. When that honor has been violated through humiliation, exploitation, or physical harm, the use of violence has traditionally been seen as a culturally sanctioned way to regain honor. Feuding in Appalachia might have its roots in the intergenerational conflicts between families who fought to correct such unjust violations of honor and well-being. Others argue that feuding was essentially the result of massive economic exploitation in the region (Gaventa, 1980). Although such feuding is no longer socially sanctioned in the region, vestiges of the underlying belief system remain, and for some persons present possible rationales for using violence.

Message to Clients:

Interpersonal violence includes aggressive acts which "intentionally threaten, attempt, or inflict physical harm to others" (National Research Council, 1993: 2). It is a common misconception that people are born to be either violent or nonviolent. All persons have the capacity to become aggressive—it is part of our biological nature. Understanding one's own violent behavior or the violence perpetrated by others is not a simple task.

There are many different reasons why people harm and kill others. For the sake of discussion, we will focus on two broad categories of violence: (1) instrumental violence and (2) reactive violence. The first category describes the use of interpersonal violence as a planned means to a specific goal—for example, the drug dealer who uses force to protect his illegal market share or the gang leader who will use lethal combat to protect his territory. Spouse abuse is often a cyclical and predictable approach to controlling another person, and stalking is employed by persons seeking to control a partner through terror. This kind of violence can easily become the primary way persons attempt to solve their problems, gain income and status, and even find love.

Others use violent behavior to defend themselves against persons whom they correctly or incorrectly perceive as dangerous, which is called reactive violence. Reactive violence can be explosive and lethal, especially when driven by rage. Drugs and alcohol are often implicated in this kind of violence, because intoxication can distort perceptions and disinhibit normal tendencies to control violent impulses. In fact, a National Institute of Mental Health study reported that persons who qualified for a diagnosis of substance abuse or dependence were more likely to have committed recent acts of violence than non-addicted persons with psychotic disorders (Robins & Regier, 1991).

In any case, interpersonal violence is a significant public health and social problem in American society and extraordinarily destructive for victims and their families. Perpetrators who are incarcerated, executed, or killed on the streets also leave loved ones who are scarred for generations. It is clear that people need to choose less destructive and more creative alternatives for conducting their lives, solving their problems, and managing personal relationships.

Skills:

Identify and practice social skills that are viable alternatives to violence. Some of these skills include:

- anger management

- problem solving

- withdrawal from high-risk situations

- changing negative thinking

- abstaining from drugs and alcohol

- managing intimate relationships

Identify personal violent behavior and distinguish between violent and nonviolent behaviors. (Persons who have habitually used violence can have difficulty making this distinction.)

Understand and apply the equation **P x S = V,** where violence (V) is the product of a particular person (P) who responds in a particular situation (S).

Identify which perceptions, thoughts, feelings, and behaviors can trigger and lead to violence.

Identify situations (places, social contexts, etc) that are low- and high-risk for personal violent behavior.

Understand how the use of alcohol and drugs can contribute to violent behaviors

Understand how the carrying, displaying, storing, and using of weapons (especially firearms) contributes to escalating violent incidents.

NOTE TO THERAPIST: Discussing interpersonal violence can be distressing and anxiety provoking for those who have participated in violent acts. Most group members will have experiences as victims and perpetrators of violence. The therapist must be aware that anxiety related to violent acts might be expressed as anger, confused responses, or minimizing. It is important that the therapist approaches this subject in a confident and compassionate way, exhibiting a calm, matter-of-fact attitude with verbal and nonverbal openness to explore this issue. Preaching and condemning—as always—will shut down group process and close off this crucial area for discussion and skill building. The focus should be on helping group members to develop ways of establishing and maintaining personal safety and respect for the well-being of others. This is a tall order, but this social skills session can be an important beginning for clients.

Group Exercise:

1. Begin by discussing the "message" presented above.

2. List the skills on a flip-chart to prepare group members for the session.

3. Tell the following story as a way of applying the above concepts and eliciting stories from the group.

    Prime the Pump:

    "Rick was a young man who had lived his entire life in the county where he was born. He had had some opportunities and some hard knocks. His father was an alcoholic and after his parent's divorce, his mother, who struggled to make ends meet, raised him. His family was supportive, and he finished high school, got a good job in the local factory, and married his high school sweetheart. Unfortunately, Rick lost his job after only three years because of massive layoffs by the company. He turned to alcohol and marijuana to get through the crisis but stopped after his wife threatened to leave him. Fortunately, he got another job in construction and was made an assistant foreman on demolition projects. This was a dangerous and high-stress job. Despite the fact things were looking up, Rick's wife left him after revealing that she had fallen in love with another man from their high school class. Rick went through the days feeling depressed, angry, and ashamed. He stalked his wife for about a week until she filed a protective order against him.

    "One evening, after a hard day's work, he joined some of his co-workers at a local bar for a few drinks. For the first time in weeks he started feeling better and less worried. He enjoyed laughing at his buddies' jokes. He spotted a good-looking woman playing pool across the bar. Feeling confident, he approached her and asked her name. From out of nowhere her boyfriend appeared, insulted him, and pushed Rick away from the table. Enraged, Rick swung at the man. The boyfriend was much bigger than Rick and knocked him to the floor, picked him up, and threw him out of the bar. Everyone laughed. Rick returned and attacked again, only to be thrown out again. This time he ran to his truck, pulled a gun from his glove compartment, and reentered the bar as he stuck the gun in his belt."

4. Use a thought map to illustrate Rick's story.

5. On the flip-chart write **P x S = V.** Ask the group to identify the personal characteristics and the situational characteristics that led to violence.

6. Ask group members to share stories of violent behavior. Encourage them NOT to implicate themselves in unreported, uncharged actions, but to recall incidents that they now know to be violent. Use the cognitive map and the violence equation to help group members analyze these stories.

7. Finally, ask the group to develop at least six specific action plans which could help them prevent, avoid, and de-escalate violent incidents through managing themselves and/or the situation. Help them utilize social skills taught in other sessions to assist in this task. Ask the group to copy these down for their own personal use, and to help them complete the practice exercise after group. While

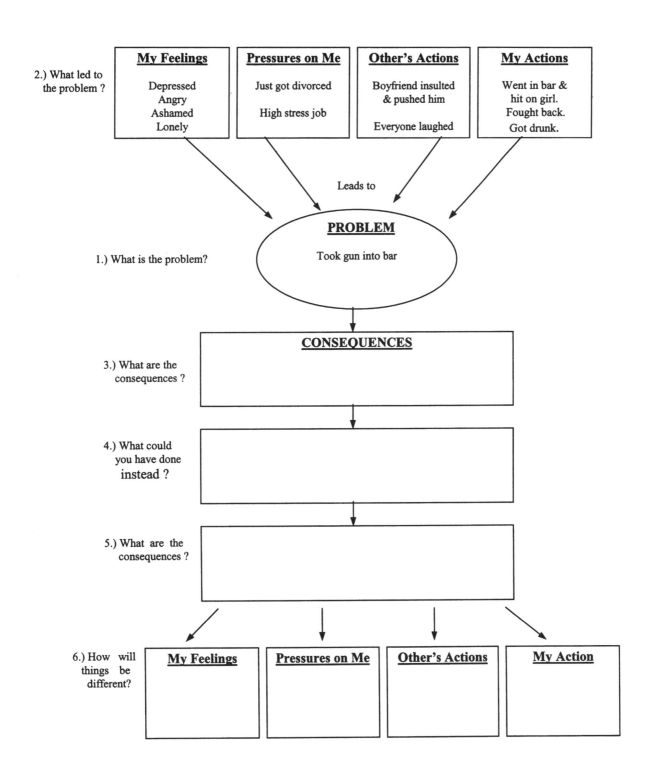

2.) What led to the problem ?

My Feelings

Depressed
Angry
Ashamed
Lonely

Pressures on Me

Just got divorced

High stress job

Other's Actions

Boyfriend insulted
& pushed him

Everyone laughed

My Actions

Went in bar &
hit on girl.
Fought back.
Got drunk.

Leads to

PROBLEM

Took gun into bar

1.) What is the problem?

CONSEQUENCES

3.) What are the consequences ?

4.) What could you have done **instead** ?

5.) What are the consequences ?

6.) How will things be different?

My Feelings

Pressures on Me

Other's Actions

My Action

it is often best to allow clients to generate their own ideas, here are sample action plans for the therapist to consider if the client needs more assistance:

- I will use relaxation exercises to slow down when I begin to want to strike out. Sometimes simply counting to ten will help me to slow down.

- When I become angry, I will leave the situation/room/building and come back only when I am calm.

- If I cannot calm myself down, I will call a friend who has already agreed to listen to me and give good advice when I am upset.

- I will remember at least one negative consequence that occurred when I was last aggressive or violent. When I get angry, I will remember what happened and repeat that to myself.

- I will not put myself in any situation or place where I have become violent in the past (e.g., bar, hangouts, certain friends' homes).

- I will lock up all firearms and other lethal weapons unless I am using them for hunting. I will not carry or display weapons to intimidate others.

- I will never handle weapons when I feel angry, upset, humiliated, or depressed.

- Understanding that long-term resentments are flashpoints for anger, I will work on reducing the number of grudges I am holding. I will talk with my therapist and sponsor about this.

- When I get worn out, I tend to become angry and violent. I will work on taking better care of myself: more sleep, better nutrition, etc. When I am worn out I will avoid any high-stress confrontations with others.

- If an angry person confronts me, I will avoid saying or doing things to increase their anger. Instead I will try to use a calm tone of voice and keep a safe distance from them. I will not use threatening words or curses, and I will not use threatening gestures. I will try to withdraw before use of force for self-defense becomes necessary. (The therapist might mention that avoiding such confrontations is not cowardice. In fact, it is the hallmark of most martial arts philosophies.)

Skills Session 8—Handout 1: INTERPERSONAL VIOLENCE

Practice Exercise

1. Identify one incident when you were violent:

2. Describe the situation you were in. How was it risky?

3. Describe your:
   perceptions

   thoughts

   feelings

   behaviors

4. How could you have more effectively managed:
   yourself?

   other people?

   the situation?

5. List five things you can do in the future to reduce or eliminate your own use of violence.

6. Do you think these strategies can work? Why or why not?

7. Over the next week try practicing the alternatives to violent behavior listed above. List what worked and what did not work. Discuss these with the group next week.

Skills Session 9: Close and Intimate Relationships

Information for Therapists:

Family relationships have long been valued in rural communities. Members of close-knit extended families often have significant emotional dependence on one another (Eller, 1997). In fact, rural people may value loyalty to family above personal betterment or even survival (Cole: 179). Males have traditionally been seen as ". . . provider, law, and protector . . . the family's agent to the outside world, and teacher to children" (Cole: 177). Keeping family problems within the family is important, and many families exhaust their own resources emotionally and financially before seeking help from others—from "outsiders." In fact, formal therapy/counseling may be the last of numerous attempts to get help. Due to a lack of trust of outsiders (Schmidt, 1994; Beltrame, 1978), it is possible that a treatment agency may be consulted only as a last resort through a complicated maze of seeking help for problems (Butcher et al., 1994).

Because family relationships are among the most enduring for many rural residents, the importance of establishing and maintaining strong, positive family relationships is very important. However, open and direct communication is not always valued as necessary in maintaining these relationships, and rural people may never have learned some of the communication tools presented here. Gender-specific roles and social groups are often strong in rural areas (Keefe, 1988), and communication between couples may be infrequent (Weller, 1965). Problems may be more comfortably discussed with peers in an extended family rather than with spouses.

The skills discussed in this session may be uncomfortable for some rural clients. It may not be a cultural practice or norm in many rural families to give or receive criticism or compliments. Community norms should be taken into consideration in planning and implementing this session. However, experience in the development of this manual has indicated that these skills (giving and receiving criticism and compliments) are enthusiastically received if the therapist first talks about how these skills can be personally helpful.

Message to Clients:

Intimate relationships are often damaged when drugs and alcohol are abused. This is due to the effects of regular drug use on people's ability to relate and to be available to others. Because close and intimate relationships are generally more difficult to manage than relationships with acquaintances or fellow workers, these relationships often suffer first and sustain more damage over time. This session reviews some basic communication skills, focusing on intimate relationships.

The rewards of effective communication within close relationships include:

1. Helping people feel closer to each other.

2. Helping promote better understanding of each person's point of view.

3. Increasing the ability to solve difficulties and conflicts.

4. Decreasing the likelihood that resentments and bad feelings will build up and affect other areas of life.

5. Drinking, drug use, and relapse are less likely to occur when there are alternatives for responding to difficulties in a relationship.

Skills:

The following skills are taught in this session:

- *Don't expect your partner to read your mind.*

  No one knows what you think, want, or feel without your telling him or her. "Mind reading" is common in relationships, especially when one person thinks they should not "have to ask" for what they would like or that they "should know what I want." Non-communication patterns can lead to dissatisfaction with the relationship.

- *Don't let things build up.*

  The more time people spend together, the more likely it is that certain behaviors they have will bother each other. Saying nothing about something that repeatedly bothers you can have a negative impact. It is important to give constructive criticism at an early point.

- *Use the skills for receiving criticism.*

  Use skills for receiving criticism to minimize unnecessary fights and reach acceptable solutions to problems. When possible, try to change the nature of the criticism and to help the other person to communicate more productively with you. You can make improvements in your life based on the feedback from other people. Even destructive criticism may contain useful information from which we can learn. Use the following skills when receiving criticism:

  1. Don't get defensive, don't get into a debate, and don't counterattack with criticism of your own. Doing so will only escalate the argument and decrease the chance of effective communication between the two of you.

  2. Ask questions of the other person in order to clarify and refine the criticism so that you're clearer about its content and purpose. By asking for more information about critical statements, you encourage straightforward criticism in ways that are likely to improve the communication between yourself and people with whom you wish to get along.

  3. Find something in the criticism that you can agree with, and restate the criticism in a

more direct fashion. This is particularly important when the criticism is correct. Instead of responding to this with guilt or hostility, assertively accept and admit those things that are negative.

4. Propose a workable compromise. This consists of proposing some behavioral change to meet the criticism.

5. Reject unwarranted criticism. There are some times when criticism is unjustified. In these situations, it is important to reject the criticism politely but firmly, in a way that is not demeaning to the other person. For example, a husband arriving home from work might angrily say to his wife, "This house looks like a cyclone hit it, and the kids have not eaten yet. I sometimes think that all you do is sit around at home while I am at work." An appropriate response for the wife might be to say, firmly but not angrily, "I realize that the house is a mess and I am behind schedule in feeding the children, but I have been sick all day and do not appreciate your criticism."

-   *Express your positive feelings.*

Many couples have difficulty expressing positive feelings to one another, especially when the level of criticism has been increasing. When there is only criticism and little expression of affection, it is hard to have "good feelings" about the relationship. Sometimes people don't express positive feelings because doing so might make their partner disregard the criticism.

Sometimes people forget that, at different times, there are different reactions to the same behavior. Sometimes there are positive reactions and sometimes, negative reactions. It is not inconsistent to talk about both of these kinds of reactions to another person's behavior. When it is assumed that "he/she knows how I feel even if I don't say it," problems usually arise. Expressing positive feelings can provide balance to criticism.

-   *Be an active listener.*

Whether your partner is talking about everyday issues (a movie or a conversation, for example) or a major topic (career goals or your relationship, for example), it is important to be an active listener.

-   Tell the person you hear what they are saying.

-   Ask questions about what is being said.

-   Paraphrase by telling the other person in your own words what you heard him/her say.

-   Add comments to what they are saying to let them know you hear, for example, "Wow, that must have been exciting!"

Group Exercise:

1. Begin this session with a brief presentation that sets the stage for storytelling and discussing clients' experience with close relationships with spouse and/or family. Emphasize that problems with such relationships are very typical in the course of substance abuse and that there are skills that can help not only to restore those relationships but also to improve them.

2. Ask clients if any of them have a story from their own experience or the experience of anyone else about what happens when people in a close relationship expect someone else to be able to read their mind. If there is no client willing to lead off, then you might try a story like the following:

   Prime the Pump:

   "I knew a young couple who had some difficulty early in their marriage because occasionally the wife, who was normally outgoing and cheerful, would walk away and be quiet. The husband would wonder whether it was something he had done or had forgotten to do and would ask her what was wrong. She would usually say, 'I don't want to talk about it.' When he would ignore her, she would get angry and tell him, 'If you really loved me you would know what's bothering me!' In fact, what was bothering the wife seldom had anything to do with the husband. Fortunately, they both learned that it worked much better if they simply told each other when they were troubled and that they needed a listening ear or a shoulder to cry on."

3. Allow clients to tell their own stories about "mind reading." Ask them to identify the hurt feelings, confusion, and unnecessary conflict that can result when individuals in a close relationship do not make their needs and wants known to each other. Some stories in this area can involve sexual wants and desires. This is a particularly important area but may be uncomfortable for some rural clients. If such stories come up, deal with them honestly, maturely, and sensitively. The group is likely to follow your lead. Do all that you can to get those clients who identify a need for this skill to make a commitment to specific plans for practicing it in their close relationships.

4. "Prime the Pump" again. Ask clients if any of them have a story from their own experience or the experience of anyone else about what happens when people in a close relationship let minor irritations build up into a major blow-up. If there is no client willing to lead off, then you might try another story like the following:

   "I remember a client I once had who was exceptionally neat and tidy about everything. He had spent several years in the Marines and liked the order and discipline. After he left the military, he got a good job as an aviation mechanic, bought a house, and got married. At his insistence, his new wife agreed not to work. Unfortunately, his wife was not as concerned as he was with everything being in perfect order in the house. After a few weeks of marriage, he began to come home to find the house not as clean and neat as he liked. From the wife's point of view it was in perfectly fine shape, but he had an abnormally high standard. He knew that to other people the house might look fine, but it bothered him that everything was not spotless and that occasionally there were things left out that should be put away. He wanted to say something, but he felt a little silly about his preoccupation and, anyway, he did love his new wife and didn't want to hurt her feelings. After a few months, he began to stop at the bar on his way home, and over time he stayed there longer and drank more to avoid coming home to what he considered a sloppy house. He got angrier and angrier, thinking that he worked hard all day, while she stayed home and couldn't even keep the house clean and in order. One night he got drunk, and when he got home, his wife started to yell at him about staying at the bar, drinking, and coming home drunk. He lost it, calling her every hurtful thing he could think of and becoming physically violent. She ran out of the house and over to the neighbors. They saw her bloody nose and called the police. He was arrested and charged with assault. She moved out and filed for divorce."

5. Tell clients that accepting constructive criticism may be the most difficult of the skills being discussed. Use something like the following:

"Many of us have the notion that whenever anyone criticizes us it is because they do not like or respect us. However, the truth is that none of us are perfect; we all have faults, and even people who love us notice and may be irritated by those faults. When someone close to us points out such a fault or shortcoming, we have a choice: we can become angry, or we can listen openly to see if there is some truth in what is being said. If we are always angry, we miss an opportunity for positive change and self-improvement, and we build up resentment in an important relationship. If we listen with an open mind to the criticism of a loved one, we can sometimes see the truth and gain an opportunity to change for the better. Even if we do not agree with the criticism, we avoid resentment and hurt and move toward a more honest relationship. Just think how much pain you would have avoided if you had been more open to criticism about your drinking or drug use when it came from someone who cared about you."

6. Encourage clients to share their stories about accepting criticism. Many of the stories may be negative: about responding to criticism with anger. Point out how things might have been different if the criticism was heard with an open mind. Make it clear that criticism is not always justified. Individuals are not always ready to change an irritating behavior, but the act of listening openly creates the possibility of positive change and avoids pointless anger and resentment.

7. Ask clients to think of things that people close to them do to make life better or easier. It can be things as simple as preparing meals, doing laundry, going to work, taking care of the yard or house. It can be things that are more difficult like standing by someone in illness or trouble, or being available in times of grief or loss. Ask them to think of whether or not they have ever expressed appreciation to those people for these supportive actions. Encourage clients to talk about the kinds of behaviors they may need to recognize and appreciate in others and the opportunities for expressing such gratitude and recognition.

8. Introduce the idea that listening is not just hearing, it is attempting to understand what someone else is trying to communicate. This is a very basic skill in all relationships.

"How would you know that one person was listening to another?"

Allow clients to mention things like eye contact, leaning toward the speaker, nodding the head, changes in facial expression, etc.

9. Ask for a volunteer who has some issue that she feels undecided about and is willing to talk with you about in front of other clients. Sit down facing her. Ask the client to begin to talk about whatever issue she is having difficulty deciding. Model the skills of active listening in your interaction with the client:

  • Repeating what the client has said.

  • Rephrasing, using synonyms.

  • Paraphrasing, using inferred meaning.

  • Reflection of the affect behind the statement.

10. After the demonstration, ask the client/volunteer whether she had a sense of being listened to. If you are very successful, you may find that the interaction with the client has assisted her in resolving the indecision. Ask clients if they can imagine themselves doing something similar in talking to someone close to them. Ask them to make a specific commitment to practice this skill within the next day.

11. Briefly review the skills discussed in this session, and remind clients about their commitment to try some of them in their close relationships.

12. Distribute Handout 1 and discuss.

13. Ask clients to complete the practice exercise, Handout 2, prior to next group session.

Skills Session 9—Handout 1: CLOSE AND INTIMATE RELATIONSHIPS

Reminder Sheet

The following points may help you with a close relationship:

1. *Don't expect others to read your mind.*

2. *Don't let things build up: Give constructive criticism early.*

    - Calm down.
    - Talk about the criticism in terms of your own feelings.
    - Criticize the behavior, not the person.
    - Request specific behavior change.
    - Offer to compromise.

3. *Use your skills in receiving criticisms.*

    - Don't get defensive.
    - Find something to agree with.
    - Ask questions for clarification.
    - Offer to compromise.

4. *Be an active listener.*

    - Pay attention to the other person's feelings.
    - Ask questions.
    - Add comments of your own.
    - Share similar experiences.

5. *Express your positive feelings.*

    - State the compliment in terms of your own feelings.
    - Compliment specific behavior.

Adapted from Monti, P.M. et al. (1989). Treating Alcohol Dependence. *New York: Guilford Press (67–72).*

Skills Session 9—Handout 2: CLOSE AND INTIMATE RELATIONSHIPS

Practice Exercise

Think about a current situation that is bothering you regarding someone close to you. Choose a situation that matters to you and that is important to try to change, but one that is not very difficult. You may want to look over the Reminder Sheet to help you think about situations in your relationship that you'd like to improve. After you think of the situation, answer the following questions:

1. *Describe the situation. (For example, "We sit at the dinner table and ignore each other.")*

   _____

   _____

   _____

   _____

2. *Describe what you usually do or fail to do in the situation. (For example, "I usually read the paper and ignore my spouse while eating dinner.")*

   _____

   _____

   _____

   _____

3. *What specifically would you like to try to do differently in this situation? (For example, "I'd like to ask my spouse how his/her day was and listen actively to what he/she has to say.")*

   _____

   _____

   _____

   _____

4. *Now, choose the right time and place, and try out your new behavior or skill in the problem situation. In the space below, describe what you said, the results of the interaction, and how the other person responded:*

_____

_____

_____

_____

_____

_____

_____

_____

_____

_____

_____

_____

_____

_____

_____

Adapted from Monti, P.M. et al. (1989) Treating Alcohol Dependence. *New York: Guilford Press (207–8).*

Skills Session 10: HIV/AIDS

Message to Clients:

Individuals who are drug and alcohol users are at greater risk of HIV infection and AIDS even though they are not drug injectors. Drug injection has received attention since about one-third of AIDS cases in the U.S. are related to injecting, according to the Centers for Disease Control and Prevention. What is important for this session is the fact that HIV risk is associated with the consequences and relaxing effects of alcohol and drug use. The most important consequences include blackouts and drug/alcohol use, which can put an individual in contact with others who are at high risk for HIV. AIDS or the Acquired Immune Deficiency Syndrome is a health problem in the United States and in the world.

The purpose of this session is to acquaint participants with understanding HIV and presenting strategies they can use to protect themselves and others from the virus. Knowing what HIV disease is and understanding personal risks are essential steps toward learning how an individual can protect him or herself. Sexual contact is the most likely route for infection for about two-thirds of AIDS cases in the U.S., according to the Centers for Disease Control and Prevention. Monogamy is a good way to protect against HIV and AIDS. However, if a person chooses to have sexual intercourse, using a condom with Nonoxinal-9 is a means of protection, although it is not 100 percent effective. Education is important for protection so that accurate information can be shared with others.

Skills:

This skills-development session focuses on two areas of skills development: Understanding AIDS, and Protecting Self and Others. It should be emphasized that this approach is educational and is not a course of instruction sanctioned by the Red Cross or another group. However, this approach is modified from the approach developed by the National Institute on Drug Abuse, and has been used for some time. The cue cards were developed by Coyle (1993) and were modified by Weschberg et al. (1997). The specific skills emphasized for this session are:

Understanding AIDS

- Usual Course of HIV Infection and AIDS

- How Does Someone Get Infected?

- What Behaviors Put Each of Us at Risk?

Protecting Self and Others

- Monogamy

- Why Use Condoms?

- How to Talk to A Partner About Safer Sex

Group Exercise:

1. HIV and AIDS should be discussed in a straightforward manner using the cue cards in the appendix. It is recommended that the therapist introduce the sessions with the following:

   "Teaching individuals how to use drug-injecting equipment is presented in this session from a public health point of view and not a substance abuse treatment point of view. It is important to keep in mind that we are not saying injecting drugs is acceptable. However, it is important to provide information so that a person can protect himself or herself if a person chooses to inject. Again, the purpose of treatment is not to help people use substances better but to stop use."

2. Ask group members to talk about the nature of AIDS and HIV. After the initial discussion, the therapist will review and discuss the cue cards developed by the National Institute on Drug Abuse.

   NOTE TO THERAPISTS: Each cue card must be discussed individually, taking time for participants to understand the points being made.

   A1 What is AIDS?

   A2 Usual Course of HIV Infection and AIDS

   A3 How Does Someone Get Infected?

   A4 What Behavior Puts You at Risk?

   A5 Routes of Indirect Sharing

   A6 What About Cocaine and Crack?

   A7 Why Use Condoms?

   A8 What About Female Condoms?

   A9 How To Talk With Your Partner About Safer Sex

   A10 Why Clean Needles and Syringes?

   A11 Bleach, Bleach, Water, Water

   A12 The Benefits of Drug Treatment

   A13 The HIV Test

A14 If You Are Infected with HIV

The Benefits of Drug Treatment

A11 The HIV Test

The therapist should also talk about the nature of HIV disease, routes of transmission, risk factors, and linkage with drug use during the cue card presentation. This discussion will reinforce points made in the initial discussion with references to issues raised by group members. Group discussion and interaction by group members is again encouraged.

The therapist will then discuss protective factors and practices and ask group members to role-play and practice discussing HIV as a disease with a friend for whom they have some special concern about HIV.

"This session focuses on understanding AIDS and the ways each of us can protect ourselves. Clearly, HIV/AIDS can be a highly charged area for treatment providers. Many drug and alcohol treatment programs find it difficult to discuss HIV and the associated behaviors, especially those related to the safe use of needles and ways to clean injection equipment. The purpose of this session is not to enter into controversy, but to present the most current information about HIV and AIDS using the public health approach."

3. Ask the group if any member has/had a relative or friend who is infected with HIV. Ask if they could talk about what they know. After that discussion, if possible, ask group members what they know about HIV and AIDS. Talk briefly about the nature of HIV, routes of transmission, risk factors, and linkage with drug and alcohol use, obtaining as much group discussion as possible. Discuss ways to protect self and others. After this discussion use each cue card to review and clarify discussion points. Emphasize points related to protecting self and others.

4. After this presentation and discussion, use a thought map after each story to map the story content and process. The purpose is to reinforce the link between high-risk behavior and increased risk of HIV infection as well as preparing clients to do a thought map based on their own experience.

Prime the Pump:

"Bill was a hard-working man who grew a little tobacco, ran a few head of cattle, worked construction every so often, and occasionally drove a truck to make a living for himself, his wife Ann, and his two kids. Bill liked to drink hard as well as work hard. He didn't drink every day, but when he drank he didn't stop at one or two. Ann had some concerns about his drinking, but since Bill worked hard for her and the kids and he never got nasty or violent, she never made a fuss about it.

"Twice a month, Bill made an overnight run to Columbus, Ohio. He would make a delivery by late afternoon in Columbus, then drive back to Cincinnati, stay in a cheap motel, and sample the bars in Cincinnati.

"This one particular time, though, Bill was feeling a little lonely and a little upset. Ann had started talking about having another baby. Bill wasn't exactly opposed to the idea, but he wasn't sure about whether they could afford another mouth to feed either. He went to a little bar in Newport to have a few beers and think things over. During the course of the evening, Bill noticed a girl sitting down the bar by herself and one thing led to another and he took this girl to his motel for sex. The next morning, Bill woke up early with a vague recollection of how the woman in the bed with him had gotten there. He got cleaned up, dressed, paid the motel bill, and left to pick up his load without ever saying goodbye.

"If he had felt lonely and confused before, he felt ten times worse on the ride home. He wasn't one to sleep around on his wife and he also knew a little about sexually transmitted diseases and AIDS. He could have just kicked himself for having sex with a stranger and kicked himself a few times more for not using a condom. What if he had caught something from that girl? If she

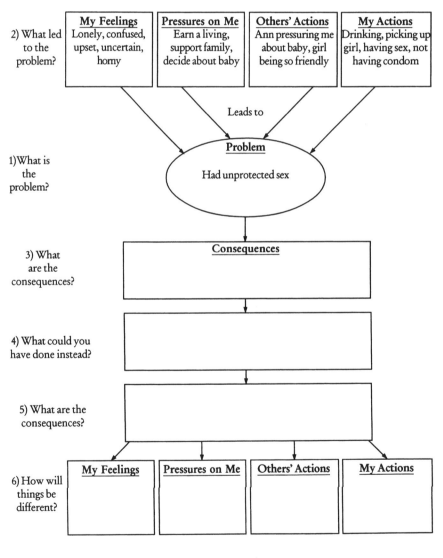

went to bed with him so easily, how many other guys had she slept with recently? How did he know she wasn't an IV drug user or that one of her boyfriends wasn't bisexual? How could he find out whether he was OK or not? What would he tell Ann when she wanted to have sex and make a baby? The questions just went round and round in his head. There didn't seem to be any good answers."

5. Use the blank thought map to map out this story. Ask clients to fill in the spaces on the map. Once you have filled out the upper part of the map in keeping with the story you have just told, ask clients what Bill might do in response to the situation. The thought map that follows is one example of a completed map. Depending on the group, your map may look somewhat different.

6. After doing the thought map on this first story, allow time for any discussion that may be raised by clients. As you lead this discussion, reinforce the points that you made in the presentation on AIDS. Some points that come to mind are:

   • You are more vulnerable to infection when you do drugs because of the effects they have on your judgment;

   • When you have sex with a stranger, you are having sex with everyone that they have had sex with, and you have no idea who that might be;

As you work through the thought map, allow plenty of time for discussion of the various issues raised by this story. Some clients may have difficulty with this story because they may want to believe that simply being abstinent from drugs will solve all their problems and eliminate all dangers. As their therapist, it is important that you assist clients in understanding that life always poses new problems for us to resolve and that there are always certain risks that all of us must face. Being informed and prudent is essential, and, in the case of HIV infection, being a little suspicious and even paranoid doesn't hurt.

7. After you have completed mapping and discussing this story, distribute blank thought maps to clients. Tell them that you want them to take the next 15 minutes or so to map out a situation from their past or one that they are likely to face in the near future that presents the risk for HIV infection. Make it clear that you are not going to put anyone on the spot or require them to discuss their map and that, if they choose, what they map will be strictly private, for their use only. Inform clients that if they want to ask advice of the group on how to deal with potentially risky situations, time will be provided. Give clients about 15 minutes to do a thought map of a situation from their past or future that poses a risk for HIV infection. Let clients know that if they need any help, you will be available. When everyone has finished, ask if any member of the group would like any advice from the group about how they might deal with risky situations. If any client requests help, guide the group process to give them whatever assistance the group can give. If no one asks for help let clients know that you are available privately to discuss any situation with them. Conclude the group.

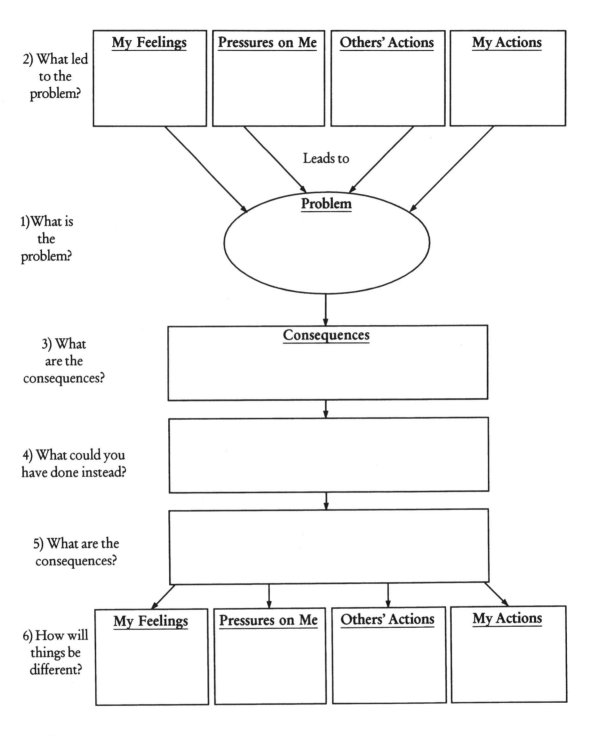

2) What led
to the
problem?

My Feelings

Pressures on Me

Others' Actions

My Actions

Leads to

Problem

1) What is
the
problem?

3) What
are the
consequences?

Consequences

4) What could you
have done instead?

5) What are the
consequences?

My Feelings

Pressures on Me

Others' Actions

My Actions

6) How will
things be
different?

7) What can
you do now?

Skills Session 11: Enhancing Social Support Networks

Information for Therapists:

A rural person's social support network is primarily their kinship network. If the family is supportive, they can serve as an effective social support network to enhance recovery. If they are unsupportive or opposed to the recovery process, the rural person will need to look elsewhere for social support. Unfortunately, all too often, there are few resources for recovery in small and rural communities. For example, there may be very few Alcoholics Anonymous or Narcotics Anonymous meetings in particular rural areas, or these groups may meet infrequently. Because so many social support systems are composed of kinship and friendship networks, it may be very difficult for a client to become involved with anyone who is outside of his sober family and friendship networks. This issue should be discussed in the group.

Another barrier for working with rural clients, particularly Appalachians, is the value of individualism (Hicks, 1992; Eller, 1997), which discourages asking for help or accepting help from others. Since a key factor in developing support is knowing when and how to receive needed assistance, group members with a strong ethos of individuality will need to learn how to accept support from others. This can take time as the person is being asked to try something that is counterintuitive and sometimes even seems "wrong," so clients need to be patient as they experiment with these new skills.

Message to Clients:

A social support network is family, friends, co-workers and other people who help each of us cope with life's problems. These relationships are usually both ways since we often give those persons support, too. Rural clients are likely to be closely connected to family even into adulthood (Looff, 1971; Keefe, 1988; Eller, 1997). Receiving encouragement and social support for recovery within the family and extended family is crucial. It seems unlikely that long-term changes will occur unless some family members are part of the social support network.

Skills:

* Committing to building or entering a social support network is a complex activity that takes time. However, the rewards are worth the investment of time, effort, and risk-taking.

* Identifying What Kind of Help You Need

  Learning how to recognize a need for help in recovery and living life without using drugs and alcohol is important. Since relationships have been primarily with substances, it becomes important to help clients find other ways to address problems they cannot handle on their own. Interdependence is the most productive and rewarding state. Isolated independence and clinging dependence are usually inadequate relational stances for adults.

- Accessing the Help You Need

Learning how to approach others and ask for help is a challenging skill that is highly tied to self-concept. For example, if a person believes that requesting help means he/she is weak, then the person will not ask for help even if it is essential to the recovery process. The whole notion of using a sponsor in Twelve-Step programs is based on the fact that such help is usually necessary. Even if a person is ready to ask for help, he or she might not know how to do this. It is important that the recovering person learn this skill.

Group Exercise:

1. The therapist should start the session by briefly discussing the ideas in the message section. Then introduce the following story:

Prime the Pump:

"Pete found that he could handle not drinking and drugging. For a few weeks he had a lot of thoughts and fantasies about using again—especially when things got rough at work. He didn't miss the long nights, hangovers, and lack of money for paying bills—but he did miss his buddies and all the people who he hung out with when he was using. In fact, he was so lonely one night that he went back to his favorite bar just to drink cokes and talk with the guys. But a funny thing happened: the jokes weren't funny and the guys weren't as close as he remembered. Pete began to figure that the whole deal only worked when he was drunk or high. When he was sober these people weren't as much fun. They wanted to talk about their problems or laugh at their own jokes. Besides they were mad that he wouldn't drink or snort cocaine anymore. After that night he never returned.

"He was still lonely. His job was very stressful and since his divorce, he had a terrible time meeting anyone even for just friendly conversation. He could talk with his sister, but she had three kids and a full-time job, so he didn't see her very often. He thought about going to church again—that's where he had made friends in the past; he had even met his wife there. However, he knew his ex-wife attended his old church and that most of the congregation knew they had been divorced because of his drug and alcohol abuse. He believed that he had burned that bridge.

"After thinking for a while, he brought his dilemma up to his sister. He was ashamed of even bringing it up because he thought he should be able to deal with this problem on his own. His sister invited him to come to their church picnic in another county thirty minutes away. When Pete said he thought that might be too far to travel, his sister reminded him that he had driven two counties away to buy cocaine. Peter laughed and agreed that it would be worth the trip. When he was at the picnic he met an old friend whom he had not seen since high school, and his friend invited him to go hunting with him that next week.

"Pete still struggled with loneliness, but he was beginning to understand that he needed to make some things happen in order to develop new friendships."

2. Ask the group what they thought about Pete's experience. Explore whether his struggle to deal with his problems relates to the group members' situations. List on a flip-chart some of the different ideas the group generates from this story.

3. Ask the group if any member could tell a story about his/her own struggle with developing or maintaining a social support network. More specifically, focus on an example where a person has a problem with which they need help from another person. Ask the group to consider who might be helpful. Consider what type of help is necessary and preferred, e.g., problem solving, moral support, helping with tasks, or receiving information or resources. Consider how to get the help you need. Make a list of the help that is available for the problem.

4. Ask group members to make a diagram of their circle of social support with themselves in the center. Take time to discuss each person's diagram.

5. Emphasize the importance of building a strong recovery network among friends and family as well as community support groups and other accessible recovery sources. Ask group members to discuss how community and family members have been helpful in the past and how this help has affected them positively. Conclude the session with the following:

    "People who have a network of supportive people usually feel more confident about their ability to manage their lives and cope with problems. Before we conclude our group session, it would be helpful to think about how you can replace some of the support you have received from this group. Research has shown that people facing a personal crisis (i.e., surgery, divorce, death of a loved one) do much better if they have support from people around them. The skills that you have learned throughout your treatment will help you build and maintain supportive relationships with others."

6. Complete Handout 1 in class and discuss. Distribute and explain the practice exercise, Handout 2. Ask the group members to complete by next group session.

Skills Session 11—Handout 1: ENHANCING SOCIAL SUPPORTS

Practice Exercise

1. *WHO might be able to support you?*_____
_____

Consider which people in the past have been:

- Usually supportive.

- Usually neutral—friends or relatives who don't know about your problems.

- Usually hindering—individuals who may become supportive with some effort on your part.

2. *WHAT types of support will be most helpful? Circle any that apply.*

- Help with problem solving
- Emergency help

- Moral support
- Alcoholics Anonymous or other support group

- Someone to share the load
- Other_____

- Information and resources

3. *HOW can you get the support or help you need?*

- Ask for what you need. Be specific and direct.

- Add new supporters—people who can help you with current problems.

- Give your support to others; it helps you strengthen your own skills.

- Be an active listener when giving or receiving support.

- Give feedback about what was or wasn't helpful.

- Thank the person for his/her support.

Skills Session 11—Handout 2: ENHANCING SOCIAL SUPPORTS

Practice Exercise

1. *Think of a current situation with which you would like help. Describe the situation:*

_____

_____

_____

2. *Who might be helpful to you with this situation?*

_____

_____

_____

3. *What can he/she do to give you the support you'd like?*

_____

_____

_____

4. *How can you try to get this support from him/her?*

_____

_____

_____

5. *Choose the right time and situation, and try to get this person to support you. Describe what happened:*

_____

_____

_____

Skills Session 12 : Self-Help and Connectedness

Information for Therapists:

Of all the supports to early and long-term recovery, self-help groups are probably the most available and commonly used. Virtually all therapists involved in the treatment of substance abuse are familiar with the philosophy, approach and value of these Twelve-Step programs. Therapists who work in rural areas are aware that self-help groups may often be difficult for clients to access and that self-help group meetings often go in and out of existence without much warning. Despite this, self-help groups are still probably the most readily available and certainly the least expensive means that a recovering person can use to support and advance his/her own long-term recovery.

Data from clients engaged in substance abuse treatment in Kentucky from October 1996 through October 1997 indicate that nearly 62 percent have had some experience with self-help groups. Of those clients who have had some previous involvement with self-help groups, 57 percent said that they found it helpful "always" or "often," and 18 percent said they found it helpful "never" or "rarely." The remaining 25 percent said that they found their participation in self-help groups "sometimes" helpful. These data would indicate that a majority of clients entering treatment in Kentucky will have had some previous exposure to self-help groups and that a majority of these found the experience helpful to one degree or another. (Godlaski et al., 1997)

Encouraging clients to use self-help groups within the context of the treatment approaches used in this manual presents some problems. Generally speaking, participants in self-help groups are required to endorse a disease model of addiction, to accept the label of being alcoholic or addicted, and to adhere to a specific program of recovery. In motivational interviewing, labels are seen as irrelevant, and clients are encouraged to exercise their own creativity and autonomy in determining the best way to address their problems. There is an obvious conflict here.

This conflict can be resolved if you remember that it is also part of the role of the motivational therapist to offer suggestions and advice to the client in a nonjudgmental and non-directive fashion. Consequently, in order to be consistent with the approach advocated in this manual, when you discuss self-help groups as a positive means to support and advance recovery, it is important that you make it clear that what you are making is a suggestion and not a prescription. Furthermore, it is important that you explain to clients that self-help groups may not necessarily be useful to everyone. During this session you will spend time helping clients understand some of the basic tenets and approaches of self-help groups. Your purpose in doing this is to assist them in understanding whether or not the philosophy and methods of self-help groups match their own sense of their experience and can be of assistance to them. It is important not to enter into arguments with those clients who do not necessarily agree with the philosophy or the methods of self-help groups and to prevent unhelpful conflict among group members around these same issues.

It may also be helpful to review the following information about participation in self-help groups, which comes out of the scientific literature. It is provided to inform you and is not necessarily intended for presentation to clients. If you think that in a particular case presentation of some of this material might be of benefit to a specific client group, the presentation is left to your own clinical judgment.

Room (1993) estimates that 3.1 percent of the adult population of the United States have attended an Alcoholics Anonymous meeting for their own drinking problems and 9 percent either for their own problems or for someone else's. This points to Alcoholics Anonymous as a significant social force that is widely recognized by those in need of information or assistance when dealing with alcoholism. However, the AA triennial survey (Alcoholics Anonymous, 1990) indicates that few individuals who have initial contact maintain that contact for prolonged periods of time. These estimates indicate that by three months after initial contact, 50 percent no longer attend AA meetings, and by twelve months, 90 percent have dropped out (McCrady & Miller, 1993). These estimates could be seen as indicative of recent change. However, twenty-five years ago, Ludwig (1970), following a group (n=145) of alcoholics exposed to Alcoholics Anonymous meetings and principles during residential treatment, reported that, " . . . *it appears that approximately 29 percent of the patients attend regularly for the first three months after discharge, but over the entire twelve months the percentage has dropped to 12.*" (211). However, those who do not continue attending Alcoholics Anonymous do not necessarily fail in their recovery. Bean-Beyog (1993) reported that only a small fraction of individuals recovering from alcoholism use AA. In a meta-analysis, Emrick (1989) also noted a significant body of data supporting recovery outside of Alcoholics Anonymous. This is also the case in our analysis of Kentucky data from a purposive sample of 1,692 individuals who received treatment for their alcoholism in 1991 and 1992. Of those who reported twelve months of continuous abstinence after discharge (n=780), 64 percent reported they did not attend AA or NA meetings during that period. Interestingly, 80 percent of those who attended self-help groups regularly and also those who did not attend any self-help groups rated their chances for long-term recovery as very good.

Considerable energy has been directed toward identifying characteristics of those individuals who affiliate with Alcoholics Anonymous. Although among these studies there is no full agreement, Emrick (1989; Emrick et al., 1993), Hasin and Glick (1992), Snow et al. (1994), McLatchie and Lomp (1992), Kennedy and Minami (1993), and Orford et al. (1975) found that the more severe an alcoholic's dependence, the more likely was affiliation with Alcoholics Anonymous. Dean and Edwards (1990) and Sandoz (1990) found that external locus of control is related to likelihood of affiliation. Perhaps it would also be valuable to examine those who do not affiliate with self-help groups. This thought brings a wave of questions and hypotheses. In reflecting on this phenomenon, Chappel (1993) suggests that it may be common "myths" about Alcoholics Anonymous as a cult, folk religion, or substitute dependence that lead to a high rate of attrition. Montgomery et al. (1993) suggest that the heterogeneous nature of AA groups may lead to initial difficulty with affiliation due to a "bad fit" between a specific AA group and a specific individual or attrition over time as groups change and are no longer congenial places for the values and characteristics of some of their members. It is always important to keep in mind that alcoholics are not a homogeneous group, and consequently, neither are groups of recovering alcoholics (Smith, 1993).

Understanding the basic tenets of self-help groups

Some of the key ideas embodied in self-help groups are as follows:

- Individuals who have serious problems with alcohol or other drugs suffer from the disease of alcoholism or chemical dependency.

- There is no cure for alcoholism or chemical dependency; no treatment will enable the alcoholic or addict to use substances safely.

- Abstinence—staying clean and sober one day at a time—is the only viable option for alcoholics and addicts.

- Self-reliance is not enough, and the support of peers with the same problem is vital to sustained recovery.

Some of the main goals of self-help groups are as follows:

- The goal of self-help groups is to assist members to avoid the first drink or the first drug.

- Self-help groups ask their members not to think about forever, but rather to focus on each day of sobriety and recovery.

- Self-help groups are not looking for perfection. Slips are less important than what is done about them. Progress is more important than perfection.

Methods used by self-help groups to obtain desired goals for their members are as follows:

- Working the Twelve Steps as described in the books *Alcoholic Anonymous* and *Narcotics Anonymous*.

- Relying on active participation in self-help group meetings as a means toward better self-understanding and support through sharing one's own experience and receiving a share in the experience of other recovering alcoholics and addicts within the fellowship. Several different kinds of meetings are provided in order to meet the differing needs of different self-help group members (speaker meetings, step meetings, discussion meetings, women's only and men's only meetings).

- Learning to use the support of other recovering group members at times of special vulnerability and need. This implies the ability to recognize dangerous emotional situations, like anger and loneliness, and dangerous physical situations, like contacts with former drinking and doping buddies, together with the ability to reach out for help.

- Developing a close, honest, and intimate relationship with a sponsor. The sponsor then serves as a kind of coach or guide in the process of recovery.

Group Exercise:

1. Ask group members how many of them have ever attended or participated in self-help groups like Alcoholic Anonymous and Narcotics Anonymous. Ask if they would be willing to share some of their experiences with the group. *NOTE: What you are looking for are those group members who have had some length of exposure to self-help groups and found it helpful in establishing recovery at some point in their lives. If you*

can identify one or two individuals in the group who have had a reasonably positive experience over at least a brief period of time with self-help groups, ask them the following questions.

- Could you tell us how you found out about Alcoholic Anonymous or Narcotics Anonymous?

- Could you tell us a little bit about your participation in self-help groups and how you feel it related to your life at that time?

- What did you like best about participating in self-help groups?

- What did you like least about your participation in self-help groups?

- Did you have a sponsor?

- If you could go back to that point in your life what would you do differently with regard to your participation in self-help groups?

There will be some clients in the group who have never had any experience with self-help groups. If you think that they can comfortably do so, ask them whether they have any questions for those group members who have some experience with self-help groups.

In this portion of the group exercise, you are trying to elicit from those group members who have experience with self-help groups some of the points mentioned earlier. If it is at all possible, try to cover all the points in the basic goals and methods in self-help groups by using the experience of group members. In order to accomplish this, use the techniques of motivational interviewing, especially selective reflection and summarizing feedback. Emphasize those parts of clients' stories that relate most closely to the basic goals and methods of self-help groups. Be careful in this process not to ignore any negative experiences with self-help groups. Use two-sided reflection to express the positive and negative experiences side by side. In doing this, you are more likely to achieve a balanced presentation of self-help groups and less likely to increase resistance on the part of clients to giving serious consideration to participation in them as part of a recovery planning process.

It is possible that there might be groups in which no one has had much experience with self-help groups or in which the experience has not been very helpful. In such cases, do not get drawn into the conflicts or resistance that some clients may express. It would seem best to move away from a discussion format and toward storytelling. Have a story ready that will illustrate the points this session needs to make about the underlying ideas, goals, and methods of self-help groups. Here is a story that may be helpful to you:

Prime the Pump:

"I once had a friend and colleague whose name was Fred. When we first started working together, he had been recovering for more than fifteen years. But over the twelve or so years that we worked together, I got to hear his story. Before he came to work with me, he had spent twenty years as a contractor for the military. About half of that time he spent drunk. Now he wasn't a mean drunk, or a nasty drunk. He was just a drunk, drunk.

"It seems he had started drinking by the age of 14. His father was an alcoholic and there was always alcohol around the house, so it just seemed the natural thing to do. Somehow he had managed to graduate high school and finish two years of college. After that, he went to work as a civilian contractor for the military. He told me that it was then that his drinking got even worse. He did a lot of traveling, and alcohol was always high on the agendas of these travel meetings. Somewhere in his late teens he had gotten married and had three children. By the time I got to know him, his oldest child was an adult and his younger children were in high school.

"He told me that he had gotten sober as a result of the efforts of some friends of his, who were recovering people. They kept suggesting to him that he attend some Alcoholics Anonymous meetings with them. At first he tried to ignore what they had to tell him. But over time, their gentle and persistent efforts paid off, and he agreed to go to a meeting with them. He said that at first, he went to meetings just sober enough not to embarrass himself. Over a space of several weeks, enough of the message got through his alcoholic haze to convince him that he should at least give sobriety a chance. He stopped drinking with some discomfort but without any serious medical complications. But, for quite a few months, he found it difficult to stay that way. He said that he went to meetings just about daily while he was at home. But once he got on the road, he would start drinking again. Since he traveled at least twice a month, he couldn't string together more than a week sober at a time. He finally felt comfortable enough to talk about the problem at his hometown meeting. People there gave him the obvious answer that, although he needed to go to meetings when he was at home, he needed to go to meetings when he was on the road even more.

"He found it difficult to follow this simple advice. He said it was partly because he liked to drink and being on the road gave him the opportunity, and partly because he found it difficult to trust people that he didn't know at these meetings in towns where he traveled on business. Finally, he said that he came to understand that if he were ever going to get any better, he would have to make a commitment to doing whatever was necessary. His drinking was just too hard for him to handle without the support of the fellowship of Alcoholics Anonymous. Once he got that message, and really surrendered to it, he got sober and stayed sober."

Throughout this discussion, as you attempt to make the points listed in the message section of this session in the manual, be careful to make it clear that participation in self-help groups is a free choice. Although, it is certainly of value for any individual having difficulty with alcohol or drugs to consider regular participation in self-help groups as part of all long-term recovery programs, it is something that every individual needs to decide for him or herself. Allow the discussion to continue for as long as you can do so in a balanced manner.

2. After this discussion has ended, summarize the basic tenets, goals, and the methods of self-help groups. Then introduce and discuss the Twelve Steps. Let clients know that these steps grew out of the early experience of the founding members of Alcoholics Anonymous and were adopted by the founding members of Narcotics Anonymous. They are intended as guidelines for a personal program of recovery within the context of these self-help groups.

3. Ask clients who have had some experience with the Twelve Steps and with self-help groups how they would answer the questions and concerns of their fellow clients. As always, keep the discussion balanced, use the techniques of motivational interviewing, and make it clear that the discussion is not a contest of right or wrong but a way of gaining information and understanding so that individual clients can make intelligent choices.

4. Discuss the value of being actively involved in self-help groups rather than simply going to meetings. You might use an analogy to drug use to explain the value of commitment and involvement. Try using something like the following:

> "You know, all of you know something about serious involvement and commitment because of your use of drugs. You can't really get seriously involved with alcohol or drugs unless you really make a serious commitment to use them. Like with marijuana, you can't just smoke once in a while. You have to commit some serious resources to getting the drug and some serious time to getting high. You also have to keep at it over time. As you do that, the drug becomes a part of your life, and after a while you can't imagine how you managed to live without it. Once that happens, you begin to experience the problems that come along with that kind of involvement with a drug.

> "Well, the same thing is true of positive effects from involvement with something like self-help groups. You can't just go to a meeting or two once in a while. You have to make a serious commitment to going regularly. And if you want to experience the full positive effects, you have to make a serious commitment to being really involved, not only in going to meetings but participating in them and in everything that surrounds them. You have to be willing to get there a little early and help set up for the meeting, maybe make coffee. You have to be willing to open your mouth and participate by talking about your own experience. You have to be willing to maybe go out after the meeting and have a cup of coffee with some of your fellow members and get to know them as people. And you have to do that regularly, over a significant period of time. It's then that you'll begin to experience the real positive effects of being a part of a self-help group."

5. Ask group members if they have any stories they can share about getting really involved in something and experiencing the consequences, good or bad. Use whatever stories emerge to illustrate the fact that it is the power of a person's commitment and investment of time and energy to something that brings about powerful effects whether good or bad. Make the point that there really isn't any magic in doing any specific thing.

Message to Clients:

Many people with histories of drug and alcohol abuse report that being connected with something, which is also called spirituality, plays an important part in their recovery. According to the principles of self-help groups such as Alcoholics Anonymous (AA) and Narcotics Anonymous (NA), the surrender of the addiction to a "higher power" constitutes a spiritual experience that enhances recovery (Alcoholics Anonymous, 59). Participation in Twelve-Step programs involves the application of spirituality to the daily lives of recovering addicts. Spirituality in AA and NA programs includes the concepts of "surrender," "letting go," "gratitude," "humility," "tolerance," and "forgiveness."

Other persons not associated with AA or NA also describe spirituality as important in recovery. Interviews with people in recovery indicate that spirituality includes a "connectedness" to a higher power, to others, and/or to nature or the universe. This "connectedness" provides a better understanding of one's purpose and meaning of life. Others define spirituality as "the human search for meaning and fulfillment in life" (O'Murchu, 1994); "being in touch with the soul" (Elkins, 1995); and striving for mutually fulfilling relationships among individuals, society, and ultimate reality (Canada, 1988).

Interviews with drug and alcohol treatment professionals in Kentucky provided the overall impression that spirituality might be more difficult for rural people, who often view religion and spirituality as the same. In rural areas, organized religions often form perceptions of "spirituality," which at times may inflict limited and restrictive standards for living. Therefore, many recovering rural addicts may feel a sense of inconsistency between their beliefs and their actions. Thus, this inconsistency may hinder the separation of spirituality and religion. Spirituality and religion have been examined separately in relation to drug and alcohol use in the literature (e.g., Gorsuch, 1995; Elkins, 1995). In this session, spirituality is not religion. However, religion can be an expression of spirituality.

Connectedness or spirituality lies behind a person's ability to be connected to others and to have relationships. In recovery, spirituality enhances the search for discovering "who we are," and the ability to draw upon inner strength in attaining sobriety. Even though teaching spirituality may be difficult, it appears to have important implications for drug and alcohol recovery. Incorporating spirituality into this manual will further contribute to the full recovery of rural clients. This session helps drug- and alcohol-abusing clients to elevate their level of spiritual thinking and explore their purpose in life and connectedness with others without the use of drugs and alcohol.

NOTE: *Introduction to the group about connectedness should include an open discussion. Connectedness can have different personal meanings to different people.*

6. Begin by telling the following story:

    Prime the Pump:

    "A friend of mine used to describe connectedness by talking about his truck. Truck engines are complex. The parts are intricately connected and rely on each other to function. However, without oil to allow all the parts to function together, they lock up and do not function at all. That's what a sense of connectedness through spirituality can do for us. My friend would say that we have the ability to relate to others. We have the ability to appreciate our surroundings. However, without the oil of spirituality or connectedness that allows us to truly form a connection with others, our relationship to them is somehow incomplete."

7. Ask the question, "What do you think being connected to something or someone means?" Discuss the responses given, maintaining focus on definitions of "connectedness."

8. Ask the question, "Are there times when you feel that your life has purpose or meaning?" Discuss responses from the group, maintaining focus on purpose or meaning in life.

If no responses are given, tell the following story:

Prime the Pump:

"A man had two sons—Mark and Billy. This man was very wealthy and owned a 5,000–acre farm. Mark, the older son, was very good-looking, intelligent, and respectful of his father. Billy, however, was less handsome, of average intelligence, and only appeared to respect his father. The father decided to give the boys a small share of their inheritance as a gift—$50,000 each. Mark drove straight to the bank and put his into a CD (drawing 7 percent interest!) Billy, on the other hand, decided to enjoy his. He packed a suitcase and jumped on the first plane to Las Vegas. He partied hard for several days. He drank, smoked, and enjoyed lots of women while gambling all hours of the night. 'Life is incredible! Life is wonderful!' he thought to himself.

"Then one day Billy awoke in a strange hotel room. The only thing he had remaining was the clothes he was wearing. He had spent his entire inheritance! He thought, 'What am I going to do?' He wandered aimlessly for days around the city of Las Vegas bumming change from the homeless to survive. He was too embarrassed to go home to his father. He hadn't eaten for days, so as a last resort, he decided to stand on the street corner with a sign 'Will Work for Food.' A local farmer offered Billy a job feeding the pigs (slopping the hogs). Now Billy had never done farm work . . . but for shelter and food, he thought, 'How bad can it be?'

"He could smell the rank scent of the farm about a mile up the road before the farmer stopped. Billy was miserable, tired, broke, hungry, and knee deep in hog manure. He sat down and began to think. He knew that his father had workhands doing better than he was . . . 'That's it.' He was too embarrassed to go home, but if he told his father he wanted to work, maybe he would let him come back home anyway. So he ran out to the road and hitchhiked his way back.

"He tucked his tail and hung his head as he walked up the sidewalk to the house. All of a sudden, his father came running out the front door to greet him. Billy said, 'Dad, I know you're probably really upset, and I don't deserve to come back to home.'

"The old man said, 'Don't be ridiculous, son. I'm so glad you're home safely, we're going to throw the biggest party these parts have ever seen!'"

9. After the story, ask the following questions:

    •   "What is it about the experience that led Billy to feel that he had purpose or meaning?" Discuss the responses given.

    •   "What experiences have led you to feel that you had purpose or meaning?"

10. Ask, "Are there times that you have felt truly connected to someone or something other than yourself?" Discuss the responses given, maintaining focus on being connected with family and others.

If no responses are given, tell the following story.

Prime the Pump:

"One way that we think about connecting with other people is through teamwork. Think about a basketball team. Each person on the team has a specific job, and all the members of the team rely on each member of the team to do his part. Do you remember the University of Kentucky/Duke game back in 1992? I'm sure that you do. Many of you can probably remember exactly where you were sitting, and exactly how you felt when Christian Laetner launched the ball that fell through the hoop that crushed the hearts of Kentuckians everywhere. That night, Laetner received a lot of glory. However, the team of Richie Farmer, Daron Feldhaus, John Pelphrey, Sean Woods, and Jamal Mashburn affectionately became known in the Bluegrass State as the 'Unforgettables.' Their first year after probation should have called for an adjustment period. However, they played their hearts out in this game—which fans later declared one of the greatest NCAA basketball games of all-time. How did they do it? TEAMWORK. Each member of the team played a vital role in that memorable game (even the water boys!). If one member of the team failed, the other members had to work harder to make up for the weak link. A basketball team is a connected system."

11. Ask, "What teams are you a part of in your daily life?" Examples may include teams at work, hunting buddies, etc. Focus on roles within these teams, and what it means to make sacrifices for teammates.

12. Ask, "What experiences have led you to feel 'connected' to someone or something other than yourself?"

13. Ask the question, "Have you ever found yourself walking alone outside? What did you think about?" Discuss peaceful scenes with wildlife, mountains, and fishing holes—what they relate to.

14. Introduce the practice session. "Let's talk about an exercise you can do during the coming week to practice the things we've talked about today. Allow yourself to experience a normal everyday activity in a different way." Distribute Handout 1 and discuss.

Skills Session 12—Handout 1: CONNECTEDNESS

Practice Exercise

The following are *suggestions* for "becoming connected":

1. Get up early and go hunting by yourself one morning before you go to work.

2. Go fishing. Focus on something you normally would take for granted.

3. Rent a movie like "Star Wars" and identify a spiritual meaning (think about the phrase "May the Force be with you").

4. Rent the movie "Platoon." Watch the movie, paying special attention to the closing scene (think about the soldiers who represent good and evil).

During the following week:

1. List two or three things that you are thankful for each day.

2. Commit to one thing you are willing to do outside the group and then discuss with the group at the next session. This activity should be practiced at least four days over the next week. Think about the following questions, and be prepared to discuss them with the group.

Describe what you did.

_____

_____

_____

How did the activity make you feel?

_____

_____

_____

What people, if any, were involved?

_____

Did you view this activity any differently than you did in the past?

_____

_____

_____

References

Alcoholics Anonymous (1976). Third Edition. Alcoholics Anonymous World Services, Inc.: New York.

Anderson, J.V., Mavis, B.E., Robinson, J.I., & Stoffelmayr, B.E. (1993). A work-site weight management program to reinforce behavior. *Journal of Occupational Medicine*, 35(8): 800–04.

Anker, A.L. & Crowley, T.J. (1982). Use of contingency contracts in specialty clinics for cocaine abuse. *Cocaine: Pharmacology, Effects, and Treatment of Abuse*. (National Institute on Drug Abuse Research Monograph 50). Rockville, Md.: National Institute on Drug Abuse.

Atwood, N. (1990). Integrating individual and family treatment for outpatients vulnerable to psychosis. *American Journal of Psychotherapy*, 44(2): 247–55.

Bachrach, L. (1993). Continuity of care and approaches to case management for long-term mentally ill patients. *Hospital and Community Psychiatry*, 44(5): 465–68.

Bandura, A. (1977). *Social Learning Theory*. Englewood Cliffs, N.J.: Prentice Hall.

Bean-Bayog, M. (1993). AA processes and change: How does it work? In B.S. McCrady and W.R. Miller (Eds.), *Research on alcoholics anonymous: Opportunities and alternatives* (99–112), New Brunswick, N.J., Rudgers Center of Alcohol Studies.

Bedell, J.R., Archer, R.P., & Marlow, H.A. (1980). A Description and Evaluation of a Problem Solving Skills Training Program. In Upper, D. & Ross, S.M. (Eds.), *Behavioral Group Therapy: An annual review*. Champaign, Ill.: Research Press.

Beltrame, T.F. (1978). Meeting the special needs of Appalachian alcoholics. *Hospital and Community Psychiatry*, 29(12): 792–94.

Benson, H. (1975). *The Relaxation Response*. New York: Morrow.

Briere, J. (1992). *Child Abuse Trauma: theory & treatment of the lasting effects*. Newbury Park, Calif.: Sage.

Brindis, C.D. & Theidon, K.S. (1997). The Role of Case Management in Substance Abuse Treatment Services for Women and Children. *Journal of Psychoactive Drugs*, 29(1): 79–88.

Buscema, M. (1995). Squashing theory: A prediction approach for drug behavior in Leukefeld, C.G. & Clayton, R.R. (Eds.). *Prevention Practice in Substance Abuse*. (103–10). New York: Hawthorn Press, Inc.

Calsyn, D.A., Wells, E.A., Saxon, A.J., Jackson, T.R., Wrede, A.F., Stanton, V., & Fleming, C. (1994). Contingency management of urinalysis results and intensity of counseling services have an interactive impact on methadone maintenance treatment outcome. *Journal of Addictive Disease*, 13(3): 47–63.

Canada, E.R., (1988). Spirituality, religious diversity, and social work practice. *Social Casework: The Journal of Contemporary Social Work*, 69: 238–47.

Carroll, K.M. (1998). *NIDA therapy manual for drug addiction 1: A cognitive-behavior approach: Treating cocaine addiction.* Washington, D.C.: NIH Publication No. 98–4308.

Chafetz, M.E. (1961). A procedure for establishing therapeutic contact with the alcoholic. *Quarterly Journal of Studies on Alcohol*, 22: 325–28.

Chappel, J.R. (1993). Long-term recovery from alcoholism. *Psychiatric Clinics of North America*, 16(1): 177–87.

Chomski, N. (1957). *Syntactic structures.* The Hague: Mouton.

Chomski, N. (1968). *Language and mind.* New York: Harcort, Brace, & World.

Cohen, D., Nisbett, R.E., Bowdle, B.F., & Schwarz, N. (1996). Insult, aggression, and the southern culture of honor: an "experimental ethnography." *Journal of Personal Social Psychology*, 70(5): 945–59.

Corey, G. (1995). *Theory and practice of group counseling.* Pacific Grove, Calif.: Brooks/Cole.

Coyle, S. (1993). *The NIDA counseling and education intervention model* (HAH pub No. 93–3508). Rockville, Md.: National Institute on Drug Abuse.

Crowley, T.J. (1984). Contingency contracting treatment of drug-abusing physicians, nurses, and dentists. *NIDA Research Monograph*, 46: 68–83.

Czurchry, M., Dansereau, D.F., Dees, S.M., & Simpson, D.D. (1994). The Use of Node-Link Mapping in Drug Abuse Counseling: The Role of Attentional Factors. *Journal of Psychoactive Drugs*, 27(2), 1995: 161–66.

Dansereau, D.F., Dees, S.M., Chatham, L.R., Boatler, J.F., & Simpson, D.D. (1993). *Mapping New Roads to Recovery.* Institute for Behavioral Research, Texas Christian University, Fort Worth.

Dean, P.R. & Edwards, T.A. (1990). Health locus of control beliefs and alcohol related factors that may influence treatment outcome. *Journal of Substance Abuse Treatment*, 7(3): 167–72.

Deci, E.L. (1980). *Self-determination.* Lexington, Mass.: Lexington Books.

D'Zurilla, T.J. & Goldfried, M.R. (1971). Problem Solving and Behavior Modification. *Journal of Abnormal Psychology*, 78: 107–26.

Edward, R.W. (1992). *Drug Use in Rural American Communities.* New York: Haworth Press.

Edwards, G. & Orford, J. (1977). A plain treatment for alcoholism. *Proceedings of the Royal Society of*

Medicine, 70: 344–48.

Edwards, G., Orford, J., Egert, S., Guthrie, S., Hawker, A., Hensman, C., Mitcheson, M., Oppenheimer, E., & Taylor, C. (1977). Alcoholism: A controlled trial of "treatment" and "advice." *Journal of Studies on Alcohol*, 38: 1004–31.

Elkins, D.N. (1995). Psychotherapy and spirituality: Toward a theory of the soul. *Journal of Humanistic Psychology*, 35(2): 78–98.

Eller, R. (1997). Lecture notes. Appalachian History HIS580. University of Kentucky, Spring, 1997: 6.

Eller, R.D. (1982). *Miners, Millhands and Mountaineers*. Knoxville: University of Tennessee Press.

Ellis, A. (1975). *The New Guide to Rational Living*. New York: Harper & Row.

Elvy, G.A., Wells, J.E., & Baird, K.A. (1988). Attempted referral as intervention for problem drinking in the general hospital. *British Journal of Addiction*, 83: 83–89.

Emerick, C.D. (1989). Alcoholics Anonymous: membership characteristics and effectiveness as treatment. In M. Galanter (Ed.), Recent developments in Alcoholism, *Treatment Research*, 7: 37–53. New York: Plenum Press.

Frank, J.D. (1973). *Persuasion and healing* (Second Edition). Baltimore: John Hopkins University Press.

Gambrill, E. (1997). *Social Work Practice*. New York: Oxford University Press

Gaventa, J. (1980). *Power and powerlessness: Quiescence and rebellion in an Appalachian Valley*. Chicago: University of Illinois Press.

Glasser, W. (1976). *Positive Addictions*. New York: Harper & Row.

Godlaski, T.M., Leukefeld, C., & Cloud, R. (1997). Recovery: With and Without Self-Help. *Substance Use & Misuse*, 32(5): 621–27.

Gorsuch, R.L. (1995). Religious aspects of substance abuse and recovery. *Journal of Social Issues*, 51(2): 65–83.

Grant, I., Adams, K., Carlin, A., Rennick, P. (1977). A preliminary report on the collaborative neuropsychological study of polydrug users. *Drug and Alcohol Dependence*, 2(2): 91–108.

Granvold, D.K. (1997). Cognitive-behavioral therapy with adults. In J. Brandell (Ed.), *Theory and Practice in Clinical Social Work*. 164–201. New York: Free Press.

Gutheil, T.G. & Gabbard, G.O. (1993). The concept of boundaries in clinical practice: Theoretical and risk management directions. *American Journal of Psychiatry*, 150(2): 188–96.

Hasin, D.S. & Glick, H. (1992). Severity of DSM III-R: United States, 1988. *British Journal of Addiction*, 87(12): 1725–30.

Heinssen, R.K., Levendusky, P.G., & Hunter, R.H. (1995). Client as colleague: Therapeutic contracting with the seriously mentally ill. *American Psychology*, 50(7): 522–32.

Heather, N., Whitton, B., & Robertson, I. (1986). Evaluation of a self-help manual for media-recruited problem drinkers: Six month follow-up results. *British Journal of Clinical Psychology*, 25: 19–34.

Hicks, G. (1992). *Appalachian Valley*. Prospect Heights, Ill.: Waveland Press.

Higgins, S.T., Budney, A.J., Hughes, J.R., Bickel, W.K., Lynn, M., & Mortensen, A. (1994). Influence of cocaine use on cigarette smoking. *Journal of the American Medical Association*, 272(22): 1724.

Holder, H.D. (1987). Alcoholism treatment and potential health care savings. *Medical Care*, 25(1): 52–71.

Intagliata, J.C. (1979). Increasing the Responsiveness of Alcoholics to Group Therapy: An interpersonal problem solving approach. *Group*, (3): 106–20.

Joe, G.W., Dansereau, D.F., Simpson, D.D. (1994). Node-link mapping for counseling cocaine users in methadone treatment. *Journal of Substance Abuse*, 6(4): 393–406.

Kadden, R., Carroll, K., Donovan, D., Cooney, N., Monti, P., Abrams, D., Litt, M., & Hester, R. (1995). *Cognitive-Behavioral Coping Skills Therapy Manual*. Rockville, Md.: National Institute on Alcohol Abuse and Alcoholism.

Keefe, S.E., (Ed.). (1988). *Appalachian Mental Health*. Lexington: University of Kentucky Press.

Kernberg, O.F. (1993). Suicidal behavior in borderline patients: diagnosis and psychotherapeutic considerations. *American Journal of Psychotherapy*, 47(2): 245–54.

Kisthardt, W.E. (1992). A strengths model of case management: The principles and functions of a helping partnership with persons with persistent mental illness. In D. Saleebey, (Ed.), *The Strengths Perspective in Social Work Practice* (59–83). New York: Longman.

Knight, D.K., Dansereau, D.F., Joe, G.F., and Simpson, D.D. (1994). The Role of Node-Link Mapping in Individual and Group Counseling. *American Journal of Drug and Alcohol Abuse*, 20 (4): 517–27.

Kopel, S., & Arkowitz, H. (1975). The role of attribution and self-perception in behavior change: Implications for behavior therapy. *Genetic Psychology Monographs*, 92: 175–212.

Kristenson, H., Ohlin, H., Hulten-Nosslin, M.B., Trell, E., & Hood, B. (1983). Identification and intervention of heavy drinking in middle-aged men: Results and follow-up of 24–60 months of long-term study with randomized controls. *Alcoholism: Clinical and Experimental Research*, 7: 203–09.

Lamb, R. (1980). Therapist-case managers: More than brokers of service. *Hospital and Community Psychiatry*, 31: 762–64.

Lazarus, A.A. (1984). *In the Mind's Eye*. New York: Guilford Press.

Leake, G.J., & King, A.S. (1977). Effect of counselor expectations on alcoholic recovery. *Alcohol Health and Research World*, 11(3): 16–22.

Leukefeld, C.G., Pickens, R.W., & Schuster, C.R. (1992). Recommendations for Improving Drug Abuse Treatment. *International Journal of Addictions*, 27(10): 1223–39.

Lewinsohn, P.M. et al., (1984). *The Coping with Depression Course: A Psychoeducational Intervention for Unipolar Depression*. Eugene, Ore.: Castalia

Lineham, M.M. (1993). *Cognitive-behavioral treatment of borderline personality disorder*. New York: Guilford Press.

Loofe, D.H. (1971). *Appalachia's Children: The challenge of mental health*. Lexington: University Press of Kentucky.

Ludwig, A. (1970). *LSD and alcoholism*. Springfield, Ill., Charles C. Thomas.

Marlatt, G.A. & Gordon, J.R. (1980). "Determinants of relapse: Implications for the Maintenance of Behavior Change." In P.O. Davidson & S.M. Davidson (Ed.), *Behavioral Medicine: Changing Health Lifestyles*, (410–52). New York: Brunner, Mazell.

Marlatt, G.A. & Gordon, J.R. (1985). *Relapse Prevention*. New York: Guilford Press.

Meek, P., Clark, W., and Solana, V. (1989). Neurocognitive Impairment: The unrecognized component of dual diagnosis in substance abuse treatment. *Journal of Psychoactive Drugs*, 21: 153–60.

Miller, L.J. (1990). The formal treatment contract in the inpatient management of borderline personality disorder. *Hospital and Community Psychiatry*, 41(9): 985–87.

Miller, W.R. (1985b). Motivation for treatment: A review with special emphasis on alcoholism. *Psychological Bulletin*, 98: 84–107.

Miller, W.R., Gribskov, C.J., & Mortell, R.L. (1981). Effectiveness of a self-control manual for problem drinkers with and without therapist contact. *International Journal of Addictions*, 16: 1247–54.

Miller, W.R. & Rollnick, S. (1991). *Motivational Interviewing*. New York: Guilford Press.

Miller, W.R. & Sovereign, R.G. (1989). The Check-up: A model for early intervention in addictive behaviors. In T. Loberg, W.R. Miller, P.E. Nathan, & G.A. Marlatt (Eds.), *Addictive behaviors: Prevention and early intervention* (219–31). Amsterdam: Swets & Zeitlinger.

Miller, W.R., Taylor, C.A., & West, J.C. (1980). Focused versus broad-spectrum behavior therapy for problem drinkers. *Journal of Consulting and Clinical Psychology*, 48: 590–601.

Monti, P.M., Abrams, D.B., Kadden, R.M., & Cooney, N.L. (1989). *Treating Alcohol Dependence*. New York: Guilford Press

NASW (1995). *NASW Standards for Social Work Case Management*. Washington, D.C: NASW Press.

National Research Council. (1993). *Understanding and Preventing Violence*. Washington, D.C.: National Academy Press.

Nolimal, D. & Crowley, T.J. (1990). Difficulties in a clinical application of methadone-dose contingency contracting. *Journal of Substance Abuse Treatment*, 7(4): 219–24.

O'Farrell, T.J. (1989). Marital and family therapy in alcoholism treatment. *Journal of Substance Abuse Treatment*, 6(1): 23–29.

O'Farrell, T.J. & Bayog, R.D. (1986). Antabuse contracts for married alcoholics and their spouses: a method to maintain antabuse ingestion and decrease conflict about drinking. *Journal of Substance Abuse Treatment*, 3(1): 1–8.

O'Murchu, D. (1994). Spirituality, recovery, and transcendental meditation. *Alcoholism Treatment Quarterly*, 11 (1/2): 169–84.

Orford, J., & Edwards, G. (1977). *Alcoholism: A comparison of treatment and advice, with a study of the influence of marriage* (Institute of Psychiatry, Maudsley Monagraph No. 26). New York: Oxford University Press.

Panzarino, P.J. and Wetherbee, D.G. (1990). Advance case management in mental health: Quality and efficiency combined. QRB 11: 386–90.

Pary, R., Lippmann, S., & Tobias, C.R. (1988). A preventive approach to the suicidal patient. *Journal of Family Practice*, 26(2): 185–89.

Pitre, U., Dansereau, D.F., and Joe, G.W. (1996). Client Education Levels and the Effectiveness of Node-Link Maps. *Journal of Addictive Diseases*, 15(3): 27–44.

Potter, L.B. & Mercy, J.A. (1997). Public health perspective on interpersonal violence among youths in the United States. In D.M. Stoff, J. Breiling, & J.D. Maser (Eds.), *Handbook of Antisocial Behavior*. New York: Wiley & Sons.

Prochaska, J.O. & DiClemente, C.C. (1982). Transtheoretical therapy: Toward a more integrative model of change. *Psychotherapy: Theory, Research, & Practice*, 19: 276–88.

Rapp, C.A. (1992). The strengths perspective of case management with persons suffering from severe mental illness. In D. Saleebey, (Ed.), *The Strengths Perspective in Social Work Practice* (45–58) New York: Longman.

Reamer, F.G. (1989). Liability issues in social work supervision. *Social Work*, 34(5): 445–48.

Robins, L. & Regier, D. (1991). *Psychiatric Disorders in America: The Epidemiological Catchment Area Study*. New York: Free Press.

Rose, S.M. & Moore, V.L. (1995). Case management. In R.L. Edward, (Ed.), *Encyclopedia of social work*, (19th Edition), (CD-ROM). Washington, D.C.

Rubin, A. (1992). Is case management effective for people with serious mental illness? A research review. *Health and Social Work,* 17(2): 138–50.

Rush, J.A. (1996). *Clinical anthropology*. Westport, Conn.: Praeger Publishers.

Ruth, W.J. (1996). Goal setting and behavior contracting for students with emotional and behavioral difficulties: Analysis of daily, weekly, and total goal attainment. *Psychology in the Schools*, 33(2): 153–58.

Saleebey, D. (Ed.). (1992). *The Strengths Perspective in Social Work Practice*. New York: Longman Press.

Schank, R. (1990). *Tell me a story*. New York: Charles Scribner's Sons.

Selzer, M. & Carsky, M. (1990). Treatment alliance and the chronic schizophrenic. *American. Journal of Psychotherapy,* 44 (4): 506–15.

Siegal, H.A., Rapp, R.C., Kelliher, C.W., Fisher, J.H., Wagner, J.H. & Cole, P.A. (1995). The Strengths Perspective of Case Management: A Promising Inpatient Substance Abuse Treatment Enhancement. *Journal of Psychoactive Drugs*, 27(1): 67–72.

Silverman, K., Higgins, S.T., Brooner, R.K., Montoya, I.D., Cone, E.J., Schuster, C.R., & Preston, K.L. (1996). Sustained cocaine abstinence in methadone maintenance patients through voucher-based reinforcement therapy. *Archives of General Psychiatry*, 53(5): 409–15.

Singh, J. & Howden-Chapman, P. (1987). Evaluation of effectiveness of aftercare in alcoholism treatment. *New Zealand Medical Journal*, 100(832): 596–98.

Smith, A.R. (1993). Social construction of group dependency in alcoholics anonymous. *Journal of Drug Issues*, 23(4): 689–704.

Snow, M.G., Prochaska, J.O. & Rossi, J.S. (1994). Process of change in alcoholics anonymous: Maintenance factors in long-term sobriety. *Journal of Studies on Alcohol*, 55(3): 362–71.

Solanto, M.V., Jacobson, M.S., Heller, L., Golden, N.H., & Hertz, S. (1994). Rate of weight gain of inpatients with anorexia nervosa under two behavioral contracts. *Pediatrics*, 93(6): 989–91.

Stitzer, M.L., Iguchi, M.Y., & Felch, L.J. (1992). Contingent take-home incentive: effects on drug use of methadone maintenance patients. *Journal of Consulting Clinical Psychology*, 60(6): 927–34.

Valle, S.K. (1981). Interpersonal functioning of alcoholism counselors and treatment outcome. *Journal of Studies on Alcohol*, 42: 783–90.

Walker, R. (1997). *Risk assessment and management: A training guide.* Lexington, Ky.: Bluegrass Comprehensive Care.

Walker, R. & Clark, J.J. (1998). Clinical supervision for boundary problems. (Submitted for publication).

Wechsberg, W.; McDonald, B.; Inciardi, J., Cerate, H.; Leukefeld, C.; Farabee, D.; Cottler, L.; Compton, W.; Hoffman, J.; Klien, H.; Desmond, D.; Zule, W. (in press). *The NIDA Cooperative Agreement Standard Intervention: Protocol Changes Suggested by the Continuing HIV/AIDS Epidemic.*

Weismann, H., Epstein, I., & Savage, A. (1983). *Agency-based social work: Neglected aspects of Clinical Practice.* Philadelphia: Temple University Press.

Welch, S.J. & Holborn, S.W. (1988). Contingency contracting with delinquents: effects of a brief training manual on staff contract negotiation and writing skills. *Journal of Applied Behavior Analysis*, 21(4): 357–68.

Weller, J.E. (1965). *Yesterday's people: Life in contemporary Appalachia.* Lexington: University of Kentucky Press.

Witte, G. & Wilber, C.H. (1997). A case study in clinical supervision: Experience from Project MATCH. In K.M. Carroll (Ed.), *Improving compliance with alcoholism treatment: NIAAA Project MATCH Monograph Series,* 6: 73–87. Washington, D.C.: NIH Publication No. 97–4143.

Woody, G.E., McLellan, A.T., & O'Brien, C.P. (1984). Treatment of behavioral and psychiatric problems associated with opiate dependence. *NIDA Research Monographs*, 46: 23–35.

Yeomans, F.E., Selzer, M., & Clarkin, J.F. (1993). Studying the treatment contract in intensive psychotherapy with borderline patients. *Psychiatry: Interpersonal & Biological Processes*, 56(3): 254–63.

Appendix: NIDA Cue Cards

Standard Cue Cards For Session I

A.1:   Basic HIV/AIDS Information
A.2:   HIV/AIDS Symptoms
A.3:   How does someone get infected?
A.4:   Risk Behaviors
A.5:   Routes of Indirect Sharing
A.6:   Cocaine Risks
A.7:   Why Use Condoms?
A.8:   New Female Condom Information
A.9:   Benefits of Discussing Safer Sex Practices
A.10:   Why Clean Needles and Syringes?
A.11:   Cleaning Points to Remember
A.12:   Benefits of Drug Treatment
A.13:   HIV Testing
A.14:   Healthy Behaviors of HIV+

What is AIDS?

- AIDS stands for Acquired Immune Deficiency Syndrome. This disease is a serious health problem in our country and around the world.

- National and Local Statistics.

- AIDS is caused by the human immunodeficiency virus, commonly known as HIV.

- HIV can destroy the body's ability to fight off infections and disease.

Usual Course of HIV Infection and AIDS

Window Period
6 to 24 Weeks

1 to 10 years
Incubation
Period

Person becomes infectious

No symptoms

First HIV Related
Illness (AIDS)

Death

How Does Someone Get Infected?

- HIV, the AIDS virus, is present in semen, blood, and vaginal fluid.

- HIV is transmitted
  - by sexual acts like oral, anal, and vaginal intercourse
  - by sharing needles and other drug injection equipment,
  - or by receiving blood from an infected person.

- HIV is transmitted from mother to child during pregnancy or the birth process. It is possibly also transmitted by breastfeeding.

- You can't get HIV through everyday contact such as shaking hands or hugging.

- You can't get HIV from saliva, sweat, tears, urine, or feces.

- You can't get HIV from clothes, a telephone, or a toilet seat.

- You can't get HIV from a dry kiss.

- You can't get HIV from a mosquito bite or other insect bites.

A.3

What Behavior Puts You at Risk?

- Sharing needles and syringes.

- Sharing cookers, cotton, and rinse water.

- Not using a condom or barrier during vaginal, oral, or anal sex.

- You increase your chances of getting HIV if you have unprotected sex with:

  - someone who has several sex partners; or

  - someone who injects drugs.

- Using alcohol or other drugs can be risky because:

  - alcohol and drugs may increase your desire to have sex and make you less careful;

  - alcohol and drugs may weaken your immune system, making it easier to get HIV and other infections.

A.4

ROUTES OF INDIRECT SHARING

1. SHARED INFECTED CONTAINER

2. USING INFECTED SYRINGE

3. USING "DIRTY" PLUNGER TO MIX DRUG SOLUTION

4. USING INFECTED SYRINGE TO DISTRIBUTE OR RETURN DRUG

5. DRAWING DRUG FROM SHARED COTTON FILTER
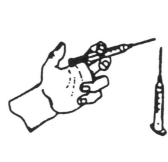

6. RETURNING THE DRUG TO SHARED COOKER

7. "EATING THE COTTON" AND "SCRAPING THE COOKER"
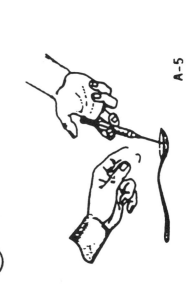

8. RINSING IN OTHERS WATER

What About Cocaine and Crack?

- Sometimes people smoke crack or snort cocaine rather than inject it. But that doesn't mean they are safe. Even if they only smoke or snort, heavy cocaine users are still increasing their risk for HIV infection. Here's why:

  - People often have more sex when they use cocaine, and they often forget to wear latex condoms or to ask their partner to wear a condom.

  - Some people sell sex to get cocaine or to get money for cocaine. This may mean they have more sex or unprotected sex.

  - Crack and cocaine may weaken the immune system, making it easier to get HIV and other infections.

- If you are a crack or cocaine user, you can decrease your chances of getting HIV by getting off drugs.

- If you can't get off drugs, be sure to wear latex condoms or make sure your partners do. Your life depends on it!

A.6

Why Use Condoms?

- Condoms, used all the way through sex, help prevent the spread of sexually transmitted diseases including HIV, the virus that causes AIDS.

    - Lambskin, sheepskin, and other natural condoms do not protect you from HIV.

- Sexually transmitted diseases often cause lesions or sores. When these occur, it's easier to get infected with HIV.

- Besides not having sex, the best ways to protect yourself against AIDS are non-penetrative sex or mutual masturbation (not oral sex). Using latex condoms is the next best way to protect yourself.

- For receiving oral sex, men should use condoms, and women should use dental dams or a barrier such as Saran Wrap.

- To reduce your risk of getting HIV/AIDS:

    Best method: no sex.
    Next best: no sex involving penetration.
    Next best: use condoms with all sex involving penetration.

- Spermicides like diaphragm jelly and contraceptive sponges do not kill HIV.

- Demonstration and rehearsal.

What About Female Condoms?

- Female condoms have been shown to reduce the risk of getting sexually-transmitted diseases and pregnancy.

- Female condoms (like Reality®) are polyurethane, bag-like devices that are placed in the vagina to catch the male ejaculate (cum).

- Female and male condoms should never be used together at the same time.

- Each female condom can be used only one time. It must be thrown out after each sex act.

How to Talk With Your Partner About Safer Sex

• Learn as much as you can about HIV. That will make it easier to talk.

• Decide when you want to talk. The best time is not just before having sex.

• Decide in your own mind what you will and won't do during sex.

• Give your partner time to think about what you're saying. Don't rush.

• Pay attention to how your partner is understanding what you're saying. Slow down if you need to.

• Talk about the times that make it hard to have safe sex. These are times when you don't have condoms or have used alcohol or drugs. Try to decide what to do at those times so you can both be safe from HIV.

• If your partner does not want to practice safe sex, ask yourself if this is the type of person you really want to have sex with.

Why Clean Needles and Syringes?

- You can get infected with HIV by sharing works another person has used. You can also get HIV by sharing cookers, cotton, or rinse water.

- Merely rinsing used works in water, even hot water, will not kill HIV. You must use bleach.

- To reduce your risk of infection:

    Best method: stop using drugs.

    Next best: stop using needles.

    If you can't stop using needles, don't share needles. Use a new needle or a needle only you have used before.

    If you do share needles, clean the needle every time before you inject drugs. Clean it the way we are showing you today.

- Do not put your needle in someone else's rinse water, cotton, or cooker. HIV can live in blood in all these places.

- Demonstration and rehearsal.

Bleach, Bleach, Water, Water

- Always clean with full strength bleach

- Keep bleach in syringe by tapping 30 seconds

- Always discard into sink, toilet, or sewer

- Bleach again

- Always rinse with clean water and discard into sink, toilet, or sewer

- Rinse again

- After you finish with bleach, bleach, bleach, water, water, <u>then</u> remove plunger from syringe and clean both parts again with bleach and water

- Never share your other equipment (cooker, cotton, cooking water, or rinse water)

- Clean your cooker with full strength bleach and rinse with clean water

The Benefits of Drug Treatment

- Can help you get off drugs and teach you ways to stay off drugs.

- Can change your life, improve your health and reduce your risk for HIV.

- Can provide counseling and support for you and family members who may also need help.

- Can provide referrals for other health and social services.

- Can provide support for dealing with AIDS and other problems.

- Even if you can't get into treatment now, you can be given information on support groups that will help you until a treatment program can be found for you.

A.12

The HIV Test

- The test screens for the presence of antibodies that have developed in your system in response to the virus.

- A positive test shows that you are infected with HIV and can give it to others.

- A negative test may mean that you are free of the virus. There is a period of time between infection and when the test shows that you are infected. This is called the <u>window period.</u> During this time, you can test "negative" for HIV but you may really be "positive." It's a good idea to have another HIV test in 6 months to be sure you don't have the virus. (Between testing, if you have sex, make sure you use latex condoms. If you use needles, make sure you don't share works – use clean works.)

- We recommend you take the test and learn your test results because:

  - Treatment is available for HIV infection.

  - You can plan a course of action that is best for you, your family and friends, and your community.

- Some people are anxious about taking the HIV test or gettings results. Our staff are prepared to discuss all concerns you may have about getting tested. Please feel free to ask any questions, so you can feel better about getting the test.

If You Are Infected with HIV

- It is important to get early medical treatment to control the disease.

- Be safe. Don't take in more virus--it can make you sicker. Do everything you can to reduce your risk.

- Some things you can do:

  - reduce drug use,

  - eat healthy foods,

  - get proper rest,

  - get proper exercise,

  - think positively--consider joining a support group,

  - get regular preventive medical care.